Most heroes seek to do their job the very best they can, to do what needs to be done. Don emphasized the importance of teamwork, always honoring the work of the group over that of any one individual. These stories are memorable and significant, told by a dedicated yet humble man. While Don doesn't seek fame or notoriety, through these pages he speaks with the wisdom of a noble leader who inspires others to remain committed to teamwork, bravery, and humility.

—Luke S. Smetters
Pastor

I found this book to be fascinating. Dr. Redden shares real life stories of his journey from being a young combat solider in Vietnam to his life as an FBI agent. With bold details, brushes with death, and even some humor, this book is a must-read for anyone interested in true FBI criminal investigations.

—Sheila Carrington
Educator

Having worked with Don in the FBI for many years, I know of his attention to detail and his desire for excellence. As a retired agent, I have enjoyed reading the events set forth in this book and recommend it for its content and for the exceptional commitment to excellence by this energetic man.

—Ron Brinkley
Special Agent, FBI (Retired)

Professor Redden's work graphically portrays the capacity of the human spirit to endure, with clear and resolute determination, and overcome often terrifying circumstances. His dramatic and compelling history further demonstrates how that same spirit may gain strength and cause him to become a committed and valuable member of the community in which he lives.

—Richard L. Benesh, Jr., Ph.D.

Excellent, intriguing reading... each story is a drama, in itself captivating the reader's attention. The detailed descriptions make you feel as though you are Don's partner either in Vietnam or stalking criminals as an FBI Special Agent. Highly recommend.

—Richard L. Weinberger, Ph.D.

I was a federal prosecutor who worked with Don for nearly ten years. His book really catches the breadth and details of a handful of his cases over a thirty-year career. A must read for all who have any interest in law enforcement.

—Paul Killion

Chief Disciplinary Counsel
Supreme Court of Pennsylvania

As an avid reader of both fiction and nonfiction crime stories, I thoroughly enjoyed Commitment to Courage. This book provides a unique look at the journey of the author from a scared kid in Vietnam to a seasoned FBI agent and the fascinating cases he encounters along the way. I have known Don for 15 years and have been regaled with some of the stories while sitting on the porch of their beautiful farm in Wisconsin. I still found it hard to put the book down late into the night, determined to get to the end of each exciting case. I highly recommend Commitment to Courage.

—Jennifer Bazan
Lieutenant
Wilmette Fire Department

As I read deeper into the book, I almost forgot that this was the story of a real man... an extraordinary man! It was refreshing to see how Don stood tall in times of adversity and stuck to his moral values when others might have folded. These characteristics are the very ones I see in Don today. Each generation produces that 5% that puts honor and duty above self... Don is definitely one of those select few.

—Steve Jacobsen

Once started, I couldn't put this book down. A compelling true story about courage, and how an FBI agent used that courage to help solve complicated crimes and bring dangerous criminals to justice. Don Redden did a masterful job of drawing the reader in, providing a fascinating look inside the mind of an FBI agent who voluntarily put himself in situations that could have cost him his life if it didn't play out perfectly. I didn't want the book to end, and I sincerely hope he writes another!

—Heidi Wright
Vice President
The Suter Company

COMMITMENT TO COURAGE

COMMITMENT TO COURAGE

The Life and Extraordinary Career of a
Veteran FBI Agent

DONALD L. REDDEN, PH.D.

Los Angeles, California

Published by
Genius Book Publishing
31858 Castaic Road #154
Castaic, California 91384
https://geniusbookpublishing.com

ISBN: 978-1-947521-05-6
LCCN: 2019900277

CONTENTS

ACKNOWLEDGMENTS

I want to thank my family and friends for their support during my career with the FBI. No one can succeed without help and no one can accomplish anything without the assistance and advice of the people around them.

I will never forget the men and women of the FBI who assisted me with their expertise. I learned quickly the need for help in complex investigations as no one person can do it all.

I could not forget to mention Charles Shor, a kidnap survivor, a successful businessman, and now a friend.

My wife Connie has been at my side for many years. She is responsible for my success as I could not accomplish it alone. She was always willing to help me, and I love her very much.

My father who passed away in 2009 was a true inspiration. If not for him, I do not know where I would be. My mother who is 96 years old, continues to be a blessing for me and my brother. You both set a good example for me.

My ex-wife who passed away with cancer, thank you for our two children and your support for me during my career and my time in Vietnam. I love you and miss you.

My publisher Steven Booth and my editor Leya Booth, thank you for being my biggest fans.

I hope you, my readers, will enjoy the stories and cases.

FOREWORD

Charlie Shor

Don Redden and I met through unusual circumstances. Sometimes I wish we had encountered each other through a mutual friend or a charity function. But the fact of the matter is he saved my life before we ever met.

In 1982, I was kidnapped by a pair of men who, in many respects, really had nothing better to do with themselves. Don was the supervising agent at the local FBI office, and it became his responsibility to spearhead the efforts to get me back alive. Despite many complications—

including my loving father's insistence on doing everything that the kidnappers wanted, which almost included not notifying the authorities at all—Don made the right decisions throughout and the kidnappers were caught and I was rescued. My experience of the kidnapping was horrible, but it could have been much worse if it weren't for Don's leadership and cool-headedness.

Don and I have been friends ever since that time. As a 25-year veteran of the FBI, Don's career has always been exciting, at least from my point of view. Whether the case was big or small—a kidnapping or a petty theft from a trainyard—and as much as he enjoyed his job and eagerly looked forward to each new day in the Bureau, for Don, doing his duty was just business. Don never wanted to be a superstar agent. He was never a "cowboy" or "superhero." The hallmark of Don's career was doing his job simply and with excellence. In many ways, he did what had to be done, whether serving a subpoena on a witness, chasing down a thief, solving a string of bank robberies, or saving my life.

Over the years he would tell me stories of his cases and adventures, some big and some small.

Within these pages you will find some of the best stories he told me over the years—including my own. Don's extraordinary career shines through on these pages. I have always admired his calm demeanor and great leadership skills, and not just because they saved my life. Don is a humble guy who lived the adventure of being an FBI agent, and loved every minute of it. His commitment to courage and duty led him to make some sacrifices, some big and some small, but he did so with his eyes open and always for the good of those people he could help and for the good he could do every day.

I'm so proud of Don's accomplishments, and this book is a wonderful example of the difference an ordinary man who is determined to do the right thing can make. I hope you enjoy it as much as I have.

Thank you, Don, for saving my life those many years ago, and for your friendship ever since.

Charlie Shor
Cincinnati, OH
December 2018

CHAPTER 1:
KENTUCKY DAYS

On August 7, 1944, my father Edward Eugene Redden became a prisoner of war. It was just over one month after D-Day. He had landed on June 11, 1944, five days after the main invasion. A member of Company D, First Battalion, 117th Infantry Regiment, 30th Infantry Division in Normandy, his unit relieved the 1st Infantry Division at Mortain, France. The next day was very foggy. In the distance, the soldiers could hear a column of tanks approaching. The commander decided that they were American tanks, and did not take defensive measures. No one else believed him, as they were sure that it was the Germans coming. My father ran for a foxhole, preparing for combat, but his sergeant told him to stay where he was. In the fog, my father could barely see what was around him. Someone approached him, but he took no action. After all, those were American troops. The next thing he knew he was facing a German soldier with an MP-40 machine gun pointing at him. It turns out that they had encountered the 1st SS Panzer Division, the elite motorized infantry unit that at one time was Hitler's personal bodyguards, and my father was captured when the Germans took Mortain.

As a boy, my father—who went by Gene, never Ed—lived in Dayton, Ohio, but moved to Frankfort, Kentucky when he was orphaned and adopted by his aunt and uncle, Mary and Roddie Redden. When he met my mother, Virginia Armstrong, she was living on a 300-acre farm her father managed in Graefenburg, Kentucky, about ten miles away. They were married for only a little while before he was drafted into the Army. My father trained as a foot soldier and was sent to Europe to take on the Germans. Without my father around, money was tight, and my mother took a job at a small store in Frankfort.

According to my mother, sometime around my second birthday she received *the* telegram. It was from Adjutant General James Ulio, and it said, "We are sorry to report your husband Eugene Redden is missing in action." (I still have that telegram today.) My mother was crushed. Nothing is worse than receiving a telegram stating that your husband has been killed in action, but this was a close second. What did *missing in action* mean? She found out soon enough. Not long after the first telegram, a second one arrived: "We are sorry to report your husband is a prisoner of war and we are doing everything possible to rescue him."

My father lived a year in a German prison camp, Stalag 12D, in Trier, Germany, just east of Luxembourg and about 475 miles from where he was captured. My father didn't talk about that time very much. I learned later that French philosopher Jean Paul Sartre was there at the same time as my father. If they met, I'll never know.

My father was liberated when the war ended in September 1945 and returned home not long after. My mother said that he was skin and bones when she saw him next. I was a toddler and don't have a memory of my father's return. There are no family pictures of him at that time.

My father didn't want to be a farmer, which severely limited his career options in Frankfort, Kentucky in 1946. Around that time, we moved to Louisville where my parents thought there would be work and a place to live. The way my mother tells the story, it took them a long time to find housing because every place they tried wouldn't allow children. Me. Dad got so frustrated that he was quoted as saying, "Is this what I get after a year spent in a concentration camp?" Somehow, they were eventually able to find an apartment that would accept them and was suitable for a family of three.

My father found a job in an accounting firm. He was a hard worker and received several promotions. He also enrolled in the University of Louisville and earned very good grades, eventually receiving a degree in accounting. My brother Paul came into the family when I was six. Dad had saved enough money to build a small house in South Louisville, which is where we lived until

I was a sophomore in high school. At that time, he took a position at Container Corporation of America as a Personnel Manager and we moved across Louisville to be closer to his new job.

Sports was important to us as a family. My father was an avid golfer and coached youth baseball for many years. My brother and I played baseball, football, and basketball, and our parents were very encouraging. They believed in excellence, and if we were going to participate in sports, we had to do so at a very high level. They also felt discipline was a trait of good behavior and it was expected that my brother and I would not cross the line. I don't remember either my brother or me testing them on this.

The church was a central part of our lives. My father was a deacon in Louisville, and both of my parents were very active in church. The church we attended was youth oriented. As a result, many activities were available, such as basketball teams. Since I was all about sports I participated in the church team and had a good time. During the summer, my brother and I attended Vacation Bible School for two weeks. For me, the attraction was not only about religion but the myriad of activities that included games and contests. It was not a struggle to go to church as we enjoyed the friendships we made there. Additionally, every year the church had youth week where services, Sunday school, ushers, and special music was turned over to the youth. We had to plan, teach, preach, and sing in the choir. One year, I was selected to be the youth pastor and give a sermon. I was maybe fifteen years old, and terrified. My parents talked me through it. I made it through with only minor scratches on my ego. I'm not sure what would have happened if I didn't have the support of my parents. Luckily, I didn't have to find out. At least, not at this age.

The church was a source of spiritual learning for me and I remain committed to my faith. My mother's brother, Boyd Armstrong, was a Baptist minister in Alabama. His son, Larry, was a Baptist minister there as well. They visited us in Louisville many times and were very influential in my religious upbringing. Besides, they were very nice people, easy to get along with, and I enjoyed them a great deal.

In the early 1960s, my father was transferred to St. Louis. My mother began working in a bank as a credit manager and my brother was still in school. I had just graduated high school, and as was expected, went to college. I enrolled in Georgetown College on the other side of Frankfort from Louisville, with serious plans to play baseball. But that didn't last long.

I became disenchanted with Georgetown. Enthusiasm is not the same as athletic ability, which shouldn't have been a surprise but was in a lot of ways. My baseball career was on the downhill and my grades were not the greatest. Something about the place was rubbing me the wrong way, and while I was passing, I feared if I did not drop out I was likely to be asked to leave. But it wasn't just that. There were so many rules, I couldn't keep them all straight. They were oppressive and, in my opinion—now as then—arbitrary. For example, religion class was required to graduate, and attending chapel two days each week was mandatory. We were assigned seats at chapel and there were other students documenting who was absent. The idea of my peers spying on me to earn points with the administration didn't sit well with my sense of justice. If we missed even once, we would face demerits. If we "earned" 100 demerits, they could kick us out of school.

There were other rules as well, and they were enforced in unfair ways. I remember one day particularly clearly. My roommates and I had just played a double header baseball game as part of the Georgetown team. We went to our dorm room, undressed, and went to the shower down the hall. We left our dirty uniforms on the floor. We fully intended to pick them up and put them away or take them to the laundry. While in the shower, the dean entered our room and saw the clothing lying on the floor. When we returned, he had come and gone, but had put a note on each of our beds ordering us to report to his office. We dressed and headed there immediately. He told us he was giving us each ten demerits for having a dirty dorm room. I was ticked off. That was the final straw for me. As soon as the fall semester of my sophomore year was over, I left.

While attending Georgetown, I began dating a girl on campus, Ann. She was a little bit older than me. Her career at Georgetown had been more successful than mine, and she was getting ready to graduate with a degree in education. She had a teaching job lined up in Louisville, and I followed her there. Ann and I were getting serious about our relationship, and it seemed like the right thing for me to do. She was living in an apartment in Louisville and teaching math in high school. I didn't move in with her, though. That wasn't how it worked back then. Instead, she asked her parents if I could stay at their house while looking for employment, and they agreed. Their house was huge and there was plenty of room. I was looking for a job, and I had a pretty good idea that I could find something substantial without a college degree, although it would be a challenge. When I wasn't out applying for jobs, I helped her parents by doing chores around the house.

Looking back, it was a pretty easy time. Neither my parents nor Ann's were pressuring me to find a job—it was a given that I would find something. My first job was with a real estate office. I was the rental manager and made $60 dollars a week. Despite everyone's confidence in me, I was starting to become desperate, and when this came along, I took what I could. I wish I could put my finger on why the job did not work out. All I can say is, being a rental manager wasn't in my blood, and I eventually had to resign.

Part of the problem was this was in the days of the draft, and I was reasonably certain that I would be called up for active duty and, more than likely, get shipped off to Vietnam. The probability of being drafted weighed on me. Of course, I was not unique in this response to the times, but that didn't make it any easier. And considering the fact that I had dropped out of school and was mostly out of work, the likelihood of becoming a soldier—with or without my choosing—didn't give me a lot of motivation. Like many of the people my age at that time, I was adrift. There were two things that kept me going and gave me the direction I needed: Ann and the church.

Ann and I attended church with her family, and as luck would have it, her father knew a member who worked for General Electric. When I asked him if GE was hiring, he told me that they did have some openings. He asked me to come into his office the next day. I had little or no experience, but the hiring manager said he would give me a chance. The position was at GE's Appliance Park in Louisville working in the range department. Shortly thereafter, I found myself improbably working as a Time Study

Analyst, which meant I was looking into ways for our assembly line workers to be more efficient. Later I was promoted to Planner, determining the number of ranges, based on sales, to be built. Some people have a low opinion about industrial and manufacturing jobs, but it's important for me to say that I really enjoyed the job and GE was a great place to work. I learned a lot about management and leadership, as I had to deal with the union resolving grievances, which was difficult at times. It was a good learning experience, and I was confident this was my career. There was opportunity for advancement, and I had a positive reputation and a good work ethic. The retirement plan was excellent, and I liked being there.

Ann's parents and mine, I am sure, had been wondering if I was going to make anything of myself. True to form, our parents stood by me with encouragement and patience, but they did not hand me anything. On the contrary, I was given the opportunity to make my own way in the world. With the job at GE, I thought I was doing just that.

1964 was a busy year for Ann and me. We married at Ann's parent's church in Prospect,

Kentucky. My uncle, the minister from Alabama, performed the service. We were already living in the Louisville area, and we rented an apartment near the school where Ann was teaching. I enrolled with the University of Louisville night school, studying business. I was working at GE and enjoying being a newlywed. But I couldn't get the draft off my mind, so I took matters into my own hands.

Not long after Ann and I married, I joined the Kentucky Army National Guard for a six-year stint. I felt that by doing so, I was taking control of my destiny, at least as much as anyone could. Ann was supportive, and understood that I was joining to try to protect her as much as possible. My father, on the other hand, practically came unglued. While he believed in serving the country, he did not believe in this war, and the thought of his oldest son going through what he had in that concentration camp for a year— the prisoner of war camps in Vietnam were said to be a hundred times worse—was almost too much for him to take. When he found out I had enlisted in the National Guard, he called me and gave me a piece of his mind. I couldn't remember him ever being that angry—or that scared. I tried explaining my reasons, but it wasn't my logic that had him so upset. Ever since the beginning of the war in Vietnam, he had had a lump in the pit of his stomach about what might happen if I were drafted. He didn't see my decision as a smart move. He saw it as walking into the lion's den. Now the question was no longer if I would be called up, but when. I did my best to reassure him that I would be okay, but by the time I got off the phone, I was pretty shaken.

Still, things fell into a routine, and for four years everything seemed to be going well. I was married, working a full-time job, going to school four nights a week, attending monthly meetings and drills at the National Guard armory, and spending two weeks every summer at Ft. Campbell, Kentucky. I was expecting to graduate from Louisville in May 1968. My job at GE was good and getting better. Ann was teaching and doing well. We were busy and we were happy.

On Friday, April 19, 1968, I was sitting at my desk at GE when a fellow employee came in and asked me if I had heard the news. Nearly everyone at GE knew I was in the Army. He said he had just heard on the radio that my unit had been called to active duty. I had 30 days to report. My heart sunk. My father had been right. It wasn't a matter of if, but when.

CHAPTER 2:
DEPLOYMENT

Coming home that night was not easy. I had been looking forward to the weekend and spending time with Ann. Now I had to tell her that I had 30 days before I would be leaving her for over a year. We had recently bought a house, and now it would be up to her to turn it into a home. A week later, my wife brought home news of her own. She was pregnant with our first child. I was excited and terrified. What would Ann and the baby do if I didn't come home? And if I did come home, would my child even know who I was? I began to wonder what other news I'd get. As it was, I had a little over a month before I graduated from the University of Louisville. I would have to give that up too. But almost worse than all that—almost—was having to tell my father I was being deployed.

I was assigned to the 138th Field Artillery, and though I didn't know it yet, we were being deployed to the northernmost part of South Vietnam to provide fire support to the 101st Airborne Division, the Screaming Eagles. Everyone knew about them. They were instrumental in the D-Day invasion of Normandy, and now they were fighting in Vietnam. I admired them and didn't mind helping them out, but it would have sat a whole lot better with me if I had been able to help them from back in the States. Tales of the Tet Offensive were still fresh in everyone's minds. From watching the news, I knew how bad it could get, or at least I thought I did. It turns out that nothing I saw on the news could prepare me for what I would encounter in Vietnam.

I telephoned my parents in St. Louis and told them what was going on. I had until the middle of May to report for duty, and by October I would be in Vietnam. My mother was upset and scared. I know she was thinking nothing but bad thoughts. Her response weighs heavily on me to this day. No one wants to make their mother fear for their child's life. But nothing compares to how my father took the news. He wasn't merely angry, he was furious. After he was done shouting at me, he started giving me instructions on what I had to do to get out of serving. "Tell them you have a bad back, or bad feet, or a bad heart. Tell them anything!"

Don't get me wrong, I was as patriotic as anyone, and willing to do my part. But the Vietnam War, if that's what you want to call it, was very controversial, and I could not grasp the reason we were there. I also knew that I couldn't "wimp out" and fake an injury or run to Canada. I said, "Pop, you know I can't do that." I knew that my father was also scared, probably more than my mother. It came out as anger, but it was all the trauma of his experiences in Germany multiplied by the fact that it was his first-born son being shipped out, and there was nothing he could do to protect me. My parents had always been supportive and loving, but they had also always let me find my own way. Now they had no choice but to put my safety in God's hands. Perhaps that's what they had been doing all along.

Those last thirty days went by so quickly I can barely remember them. By May 20, 1968, I was in Killeen, Texas, training in earnest at Fort Hood next to experienced units like the 7th Cavalry. I would be there through September and deploying to Vietnam in October. They were teaching us how to survive in combat. There was much to learn. Our artillery unit had trained together for the last four years, but this was something else. It was different and more intense every day. We were under the watchful eyes of regular army soldiers who had served in combat before. The instructors had experience and were able to teach us how to fire the artillery guns, perfect our use of personal weapons, learn the culture of Vietnam, and even created simulations of walking through a jungle filled with booby traps. The Viet Cong—the non-uniformed guerrilla soldiers in South Vietnam supporting the North Vietnamese regular army—were masters at setting up ambushes and traps. They were known for creating hidden pits filled with sharp "punji" sticks covered with manure so that if you stepped on one not only would you be wounded but it would immediately become infected. There was more, but I don't want to recall it. Suffice to say, it was scary.

At that point I was an E-6 Specialist Section Chief—roughly a sergeant first class—and I was tapped to head up the meteorological unit. This was not what I had been training for in the National Guard, and I had to learn new skills. The meteorological unit determines local weather between the artillery batteries and the targets and calculates wind correction and other factors that are fed into fire control calculations to help make artillery fire more accurate.

I knew most of the guys in the 138th, and it was good to have some familiar faces in the barracks and during training. It was hard, though, watching some of the men I had admired during weekend drills in Louisville completely lose it. There's only so much I could say to a crying man, especially when I shared his fears down to my toes and didn't have a clue how to make any of it easier or better for him or me. We didn't have a lot of time to think though. They kept us busy with physical training, classes, and weapons practice. As my confidence grew, the lava in the pit of my stomach cooled a little, but not nearly enough.

The time for us to ship out to Vietnam was approaching too quickly. In September, every soldier was allowed to travel home for two weeks. This was done in shifts, and by the last week of the month we had to report for duty. Our departure date was October 1, 1968. I had been released to travel home earlier than the other guys in the unit because Ann, who was pregnant, had been making statements about not wanting to have the baby, which was due in the winter. I went home to calm her as much as I could, which was not easy because I was full of anxiety myself. That week was too short. It was hard leaving again, but I returned to Texas and prepared to deploy.

The time arrived and we packed our belongings into duffle bags that we could barely lift. No one slept a wink that night. We were put on buses at 3:00am to go to the airport. As we were leaving the post, the Army band started playing "My Old Kentucky Home." What a thing to have to listen to as we were shipping out, maybe never to see our homes again. It was very emotional. I think they were trying to get us to start grieving early and get it out of our systems. If that was their goal, it didn't work, at least not on me.

The flight to Vietnam was unremarkable but for the fact that it was so long. Twenty-three hours later, we arrived at Da Nang. When we stepped out onto the tarmac, we knew that there would be no turning back. I think we were all in a state of shock. We walked across the airport apron to another waiting plane, a C-130 transport, which took us to a place called Phu Bai. I had never heard of that place before but it nevertheless became my home for the first month I was in country.

The flight from the States had been on a commercial airliner, with toilets, actual seats, and flight attendants. The C-130 had none of those luxuries. We sat on the floor in rows and held onto straps. Someone told us as we were boarding to watch out for the takeoff, since the pilot was going to ascend at an extreme angle to avoid sniper fire from the Viet Cong. Boy, that guy wasn't kidding. Sure enough, the pilot took off like a rocket, and descended into Phu Bai like a rock. It was not the friendly skies.

Phu Bai Combat Base was essentially an airfield in the north end of South Vietnam, just south of a coastal city named Hue. It was never far from the fighting, but it was safe enough. I think that's why they sent us there first. To get used to being shot at without putting us in the direct line of fire.

On the other hand, it wasn't exactly summer camp either. It was hardly what anyone would consider paradise. We lived in "hooches," kind of a hut, and slept on cots.

The latrine was an experience unto itself, as was pulling latrine duty, which included pumping out the crap and setting the contents on fire to get rid of the stuff. Needless to say, pulling latrine duty was punishment.

There were no showers available during most of the time we were there. Considering how hot and muggy it was in Vietnam, this was a real hardship. I said most because as the end of our first month in country came to a close and we were about to be shipped out to God only knew where, suddenly makeshift showers appeared. I wouldn't be surprised if that was on purpose. The Army was not above playing games like that.

I continued to have mixed feelings about serving in this war. I was scared but I was there for the duration and had a job to do. That didn't mean that I had to like it. As time passed, I became bitter. I did not know the purpose of it all. Most of us were simply trying to survive long enough to go home. I remember listening to General Westmorland, the commander of all U.S. forces in Vietnam, in a press conference. He was telling the American people that we were winning the war. And I thought, who is he kidding? We weren't winning anything. "What's he been smoking?" I said. It was ridiculous. Propaganda. It did nothing to help my attitude toward being there at all.

The first two weeks in Phu Bai were relatively quiet as far as any combat goes. We kept busy setting up our equipment, writing letters, and trying to sleep. My unit consisted of two teams and they worked twelve-hour days. We were responsible for gathering data regarding weather, wind speed and direction, atmospheric pressure, and temperature. The data we generated was provided to the Fire Direction Center (FDC) and used for aiming and accuracy. Our unit was composed of headquarters, maintenance, and three firing batteries. The firing batteries, A, B, and C, were situated in locations where they could best protect the base and assist soldiers requiring firepower.

In the third week in Phu Bai, we were attacked with rockets. This was the first time we were hit while I was there. They sent in five or six rockets. After the first one exploded, we all knew what was happening and hightailed it to the perimeter where there were bunkers we jumped into for cover. The rockets from the enemy were 122 millimeters—which is almost five inches in diameter—and very loud and powerful, but thank goodness the Viet Cong were not up to date with equipment that could help them hit their target. They just eyeballed it and sent the rocket in.

After the all clear was sent, we went back to our hooch and tried to relax. Within a few days we were hit again. This was a little different than the first time. The enemy sent a few rockets our way and then we could hear explosions from mortars. When mortars are heard, you can bet the enemy is close. The call went out for help and Cobra gunships were in our area in a few minutes. They fired hundreds of ammo rounds outside the perimeter where the Viet Cong were positioned.

Battery A was ordered to fire artillery rounds in the area around the perimeter. My unit had just finished providing the batteries with our report on weather conditions and wind. We did this four times each day, providing up to date information to FDC. Sergeant Roscoe Sharp had the duty that night and was in charge of the data we provided right before the shooting started. After the data was complete, he gave it to me to check for accuracy. It looked good to me. The guns were in position and ready to fire using data we provided. The order was given, and the artillery round was on the way. We could hear the explosion. It was near the perimeter, but just outside, or so we thought.

We soon found out the round hit inside the perimeter into a bunker occupied by a sergeant and another soldier. It was a direct hit, and nothing was left. Our battery was ordered to cease fire. It was terrible and everyone grieved for the loss. It was bad enough we lost two men from friendly fire, now we had to determine what went wrong. I can tell you I was scared to death as I was thinking about our data. It's crucial that it be accurate, and any mistake could be catastrophic. I knew that the army was hellbent to find someone to blame. I retrieved our report and went over it with a fine-tooth comb and could not find any errors. I did not think I would as Sergeant Sharp was very conscientious about his work. Thank goodness we did not make any mistakes because I had to produce the report for the investigative team to review.

The findings of the investigation were terrible, just as gut wrenching as the death of the two soldiers. It was found to be an error of the placing of the aiming stakes that are put out in front of the guns. I didn't know the soldier responsible, but I know he was sick with guilt and felt horrible as no one wants to be in that position. Sadly, I soon learned that forty percent of the deaths of our soldiers came as a result of friendly fire. Not a good thought.

A few days later, I was called to the Captain's office. He told me I was going to be sent to

Landing Zone (LZ) Nancy just south of the demilitarized zone (DMZ) for the remaining eleven months. This was a regular army unit and they were without a Meteorological Section Chief. I did not know what to say, so I did not say anything. I knew it would not make any difference. Luckily, I was able to bring Sergeant Sharp with me. I packed up my belongings, put them in a duffle bag, and off to LZ Nancy we went.

CHAPTER 3:
LANDING ZONE NANCY

I was both happy and sad to leave Phu Bai. Sad
being separated from friends but happy to get
away from the sergeant who had also been our
trainer while at Ft. Hood. He was regular army
and thus a career soldier. National Guard troops
like mine were and still are called "weekend
warriors" by regular army types. The National
Guard is as much a part of the Army as the
regulars. In fact, we were second string ahead of
the reserves. Nevertheless, the regular army liked
to ridicule us, and that trainer sergeant enjoyed

every minute of what he put us through. We had no choice but to tolerate this, and I was glad to be getting away from him. I found out later he had volunteered to deploy with us to Vietnam. What an idiot. He was rude, obnoxious, and a few other things I'd prefer not to put into print.

Sergeant Sharp and I arrived at LZ Nancy that afternoon. The base was carved out of the jungle by combat engineers in 1968, soon after the Tet Offensive. It was located a few kilometers from Quang Tri Province which had been overrun during Tet. We were as close to the front lines as we could get without being in the middle of it.

We went to the command center and met the Captain and First Sergeant. They both welcomed us and the first thing out of their mouths was "if Charlie wants you, Charlie will get you." A sobering thought for sure. They told me that, in addition to my duties as section chief of my unit, I was also in charge of a section of the perimeter. We had no choice but to make the best of it.

Sargent Sharp and I settled in and went to meet the soldiers who were in the meteorological section. All were regular army who had been drafted or enlisted. They were generally easy to get along with, as none of them were career army types like that terrible training sergeant. The first few days were spent getting to know everyone, cleaning our rifles, and reinforcing sandbags around the hooch. It was a good thing we did. About four days after we arrived, we were attacked after dark with a barrage of rockets. I could not believe what was happening. The chaos was overwhelming. Unlike supersonic projectiles (bullets, artillery fire, etc.), you could hear the incoming rockets before they arrived, which scared the hell out of us. The sound of the explosions was deafening. LZ Nancy was not a large area, and when a rocket hit, the entire compound was affected. As I was running to get to the bunker near the perimeter, I thought, "Wow, Phu Bai was a piece of cake compared to this." The LZ was hot—not just the weather— and even if I survived, I still had eleven months to go before I could get out of there. With all the combat in the area, there was no guarantee I would see home again.

The morning after the fireworks we surveyed the damage. One of the rockets had taken out a large area of sandbags that were protecting one of our sleeping quarters. I found a piece of shrapnel from the rocket and picked it up. It was nasty and if anyone had been hit with this, it would have been lights out. I kept it and brought it home with me as a reminder. (I still have it to this day.) Of course, we needed to get more sandbags to replace the ones lost. I took four of my men and drove to an area outside the gate where we could fill the bags. We had two soldiers standing guard, and it turned out that we had every good reason to be on the lookout. The bags were filled, and we returned to the LZ. As we approached the camp, we noticed several GIs standing near the gate, and it was open. As we came closer, we could see an individual standing with his hands behind his head. The GIs had their rifles pointed at him. We stopped and realized this was a North Vietnamese regular army soldier. He told the interpreters he had been hiding in the bushes near the gate we had passed through that morning. My thoughts were that he could have taken us all out if he chose to. Instead, he told the interpreters, he wanted to give up. He was blindfolded, cuffed, and whisked off to the command post. That was not only strange but a little too close for comfort.

During the next several months, we were hit randomly. Every other day, every week—there was no way to predict it. One thing I learned was that in combat you make friends quickly. There is no such thing as an enemy on our side. We had to stay together and help each other. One night we were getting hit hard. I was running down to the perimeter, looked back over my shoulder and could see the rockets being launched from a hill just west of us. Because I did not know where the next one was going to hit, I dropped to the ground instead of continuing to the bunkers. While lying there, every bone in my body was shaking. I put my head down and thought, "This is it, I am done, I am not going to make it. I am never going to see my daughter." There is a macho myth that real men are not supposed to be scared in combat. I can tell you that is crap intended to make the rest of us feel small. Combat changes you. Your heart pounds, and you experience fear and tunnel vision. Nothing I can say here can adequately describe it. I don't recommend finding out what combat is like if it can be avoided.

Eventually, I didn't die, and I continued down to the bunker. The rockets continued and air support was requested. Soon, but not soon enough, two fighter jets—Air Force F-4 Phantoms—were in our territory. We watched as the two pilots dropped napalm over the hillside. It was some sight to see the pilots dive in and drop their ordnance. Soon the rockets were silent, but the jets continued their mission. Many of us got out of our bunkers and watched the airshow. It was quite a sight and we were jumping up, yelling, elated the enemy rockets had stopped. I wish I could have been able to thank those pilots for their help.

One time we were hit for ten straight days and nights. I think the NVA (North Vietnamese regular army) just wanted to make us miserable. We had little or no sleep and ate when we could. We went through a lot of C-rations—precooked meals in boxes that tasted like the cardboard that contained them but any food was good enough. Our guns would return fire, but we never knew if they were successful. I thought for sure the Vietnamese were going to try to overrun us.

We were sprayed weekly with Agent Orange. This was a defoliant meant to kill off the jungle so we could see the enemy. It was terrible and later was found to be an extreme hazard for the troops. Among the many illnesses it caused, cancer was number one. I found out after doing some research, forty thousand gallons of Agent Orange were dropped on LZ Nancy. We could smell it every time it was spread on us. The U.S. Army did not do us any favors with this horrible chemical.

One morning in Vietnam, as I was shaving, I looked in the mirror and my face was covered with weird marks. I had no idea what was going on and the first thing I thought was that I might be held over and not be able to go home when it was time. We knew about several soldiers who were not allowed to leave the country because they may have been contagious. I went immediately to the medic and even he could not tell me anything. He gave me some special soap and told me to wash my face twice a day for a week to see if it would clear up. It worked. Boy was I relieved.

The hours, days, weeks, and months passed with pretty much the same routine of sporadic fire from the enemy. I would like to say before we knew it, but Roscoe and I were fully aware of the approach of our last fifteen days in country. On that night, so close to our going home, we were hit big time. All I could think was "Oh no." I ran to the bunker, made sure everyone had ammo, and hunkered down. Soon there was a lull and complete silence, which was strange. We sat for about one hour with nothing going on. We kept the flares going, making sure we could see.

After some time, I was ordered to the command post. The Captain wanted my team to go on a night patrol around the perimeter, since I was in charge of the perimeter that night. Fifteen days to go and he wanted me to take a night patrol? I did not say that to him, but I thought it. He said to get eight men to walk the perimeter. I went to back to my unit and told them what I had been asked to do. I told them no one else had to go. Roscoe Sharp said, "If you are going, I am going." I could have hugged him. I had eight men willing to go right away. I asked for an armored personnel carrier (APC) and plenty of flares to light our way. I was loaded down with ammo and grenades, as all of us were. I had a round in the chamber and the safety was off. I said to Roscoe, "If so much as a water buffalo jumps up, he is going down." We followed the APC and thank goodness we did not see one thing. By the time we returned to our hooch, I was wringing wet with sweat and grateful for all who went with me.

Finally, the time had arrived to get off LZ Nancy. Roscoe and I were leaving the same day. The Captain ordered a formation for the unit before we left. He called our names out and asked for us to step up to the front of the unit. He read a proclamation and awarded Roscoe a medal of commendation for his service. He then read a proclamation and awarded me a Bronze Star for meritorious service against a hostile force. While the recognition was nice, I was far more pleased and grateful to be almost home. I was one of the lucky ones.

CHAPTER 4:
HOME AGAIN

Boarding the plane in Da Nang was truly joyful. I could not believe we were going home. My daughter was ten months old and I could not wait to meet her. We flew to the Philippines, then to Seattle, and finally to Louisville, Kentucky. The flight crew was great, very accommodating and seemed to be just as excited as we were to get us home. It was around 4:00 AM when we touched down in Louisville. As we approached the hanger, we could see throngs of people cheering our return, even though it was early in the morning. The news we were coming home was front page in the Louisville newspaper. The pilot and crew all stepped out and applauded us and thanked us for our service and for being so polite during the flight.

The crew was getting ready to open the doors when some stupid officer began giving everyone a speech. You could hear the people hollering and cheering outside and this idiot was droning on. I wanted to say get the hell out of the way. I'm sure everyone on the plane felt the same. Eventually, he was drowned out and the doors were opened. I was the fifth person to come down the steps. It felt good to be on American soil again. There were so many people, but I could not see anyone I knew. Suddenly, Ann ran to me and jumped into my arms. Someone was holding my daughter and gave her to me. She cried and I did too. My mother, father, and brother had driven from St. Louis to greet me and I was happy to see them as well. My dad was especially glad I was home. I can't imagine his relief that I had made it back safely, but if I had to guess, I would say it was something equivalent to my own joy.

My father drove us home and it seemed no one knew what to say; there was little conversation.

I was sure my father had told everyone in my family of things not to mention.

I was thankful yet sorry for the ones that did not return. The war and the loss and the stupidity of it all still affects me. I travel to Washington D.C. each year to visit my father's gravesite in Arlington Cemetery, and the Vietnam Memorial. As I walk up and down the Memorial, I ask myself, why?

While I was in Vietnam, money had been very tight and we almost lost the house. The army, in their infinite wisdom, paid me $65 per *month* as combat pay. I had been making more than $65 per *week* before leaving. It was ridiculous. Ann and I were lucky to have kept our house.

I was not one to sit around and feel sorry for myself. I had been through hell and survived, but I knew that I had to get back to work quickly as money was tight. One week after arriving home from Vietnam, I drove to General Electric. I was very familiar with the operation and my transition back into the job was not a difficult task. I met with many of my previous co-workers and all welcomed me. Many asked why I did not take more time to relax from the ordeal. I told them I needed to go back to work.

The general manager was told that I was in the building and he met me in the hallway and asked me to come to his office. I told him I needed a job. He said he would find me a position and would compensate me for the time I was away, which was really nice of him.

The very next day he telephoned me and said he wanted me to be a foreman supervising three assembly lines on second shift. He picked the second shift because he knew I needed money and the pay was ten percent higher then. Things were working out very well. I was convinced I was going to retire from this company.

Most everyone in the range department already knew me and were very nice to me. I had heard of the many demonstrations criticizing the war in Vietnam and the negative comments made to veterans. Soldiers were spit on, cursed, and called baby killers in many cities around the country. Not here. I did not hear one negative comment about my time in Vietnam. On the contrary, people were very supportive of the military and my service. My only concern was answering questions. Some would ask if I ever killed anyone. I really didn't know how to respond. Others would ask if we were ever shot at. I wanted to say, but I did not: "Do you think I was on vacation?" I struggled with the curiosity for a while. There are still some questions I won't answer.

I was slowly getting into the routine of civilian life, thinking all the while of the difficult tasks we were faced with in Vietnam. There, personal hygiene was challenging. As much as you tried, it was difficult to simply brush your teeth, shave, and keep your body clean. Being home and having access to showers and toilets was a godsend.

CHAPTER 5:
DREAMING OF THE FBI

After I got home it was relatively easy to return to much of my routine, but going to church was a different matter. It took me a few weeks to get back to my home church. It was a small Baptist church with an interim pastor. My wife and her family were members and very religious, so I had people there with me who understood what I had gone through—as much as anyone who wasn't there could. I was experiencing restlessness for some reason. I wanted to go to church but did not want to participate; just sit, listen, and think.

Church had always been important to me, but more for the social aspects. I'm still quite religious and go to church regularly to this day, but that doesn't mean that I go for the same reasons as everyone else. Church is very personal for me. It is the people there that draw me back.

Prior to Christmas 1969, I noticed a new couple was showing up at most of the services. They seemed friendly enough and I introduced myself. Tom Carpenter was the husband; for the life of me I cannot remember his wife's name. At a social function at church, I struck up a conversation with Tom. He told me he was an FBI agent and I was impressed. He looked the part: athletic, well dressed, and very friendly. I was not sure what to ask him about his job. On the other hand, he began quizzing me about Vietnam and was very curious about my service. He was good at asking questions that I was willing to answer, and we had a good conversation. In response, I began asking him about the FBI. The more he told me, the more interested I became. Not in joining the FBI—that was the furthest thing from my mind. But it was fun and kind of fascinating to talk with someone with such a fantastic job.

In January 1970, Tom asked if I would be interested in applying to the FBI. I thought he was out of his mind. Agents had to have a college degree. I still had one more semester to go for my bachelor's in business, which would be in the spring semester later that year. I was all set with my career at GE, but something about becoming an agent intrigued me. I thought about this for some time, and finally worked up my courage to talk to Ann about it. She was not overly excited. Not exactly down on the idea, but she didn't see it as a step up either. I think she was worried that it would be dangerous, and besides, my working in law enforcement was a completely new idea. Besides, I was not sure I would make it through the application process anyway The whole thing was a big risk and neither one of us was sure it was the right move.

Tom wanted me to apply, go through all the steps, tests, physical exam, and interviews, to be ready to go after I graduated. I agreed thinking, even if I do not make it, I still have a good job. I was very busy with work at GE as a shift leader. Because I was working the second shift, however, I was able to schedule my interviews in the mornings. I felt a little disloyal to the folks at GE by looking for another "job" with the FBI, but not so guilty that I didn't do it.

The written tests were tough. English, math, government, general knowledge. It was like being on the TV game show Jeopardy. The background checks were very important to the Bureau, and they left no stone unturned. They interviewed family, friends, neighbors, schoolmates, teachers, and even my employer, although they left GE for last.

Each office had a recruiting agent, and I interviewed with him for a few hours. He asked questions about my personality, how I would handle certain situations, how I would handle personal interactions, anything and everything the FBI could think of. I must have done well, because they didn't reject me right then and there.

The time came for me to take my written exam. Because I was working the second shift at GE, I usually got home late at night. On the day before the exam, there was a problem with the assembly line and I was at the plant much later than usual. The test was very early the next morning. Add to that the fact that I was quite nervous, and I barely got any sleep that night, probably less than an hour total. When I presented myself at the Louisville FBI office for the test, I was a wreck. Showered, shaved, and caffeinated, but still not on my best game by a long shot.

I sat down and the examiner, a gaunt man who looked very much the role of schoolmaster, handed me my test and the only acceptable tools I was allowed: four pencils and a very small metal pencil sharpener. I stared at the test, unsure how to proceed. I was in no condition to do much more than sleep in my chair. Nevertheless, I did my best.

I finished the test and looked at the clock. It was much too early. I had at least another hour to go on the allotted time. I considered going over my answers again, but by this point the questions and answers all looked the same. It would do me no good to check my work, and I had no desire to be there one more minute than necessary, so I stood up and approached my schoolmaster. Handing him my test, I stood there waiting for further instructions.

He flipped through my exam, checking page after page, and it was clear that he didn't like what he saw. Then he did something that I would have never anticipated. He said, "Care to explain?"

I knew an opportunity when I heard one. I carefully laid out my case for why I was not at my best. I told him about the assembly line at GE, my rough night sleeping, my nerves, the four cups of coffee I had consumed before arriving, and then I added how Tom Carpenter was counting on me to pass these tests. I told him what it would mean to me to become an FBI agent, and what it would mean to my family. Eventually I wound down, and took a deep breath.

The agent continued to stare into my face in disbelief. Then he looked away. I figured I was dismissed. I turned to leave. The agent cleared his throat behind me and said my name. I turned to see him holding out a handwritten piece of paper. I approached and took it. It had a phone number and a name written on it. "Tell the office," he said, "that you have been granted a retest, and give them my name."

Astonished, I took the paper and thanked him. Once again I turned to go. "Redden," he said. I looked back. "Get some sleep next time. You'll do fine."

I came back a week later with a good night's sleep under me. It took the whole four hours to complete the test, but I made it under the wire. This time, the agent—I wish I could remember his name, as it was the same man—looked at my test, flipping from page to page. He cleared his throat like before and this time said, "You'll be hearing from us. Dismissed." I left gratefully.

My last interview was with the Special Agent in Charge (SAC) of the Louisville office. We had a good conversation. He seemed particularly interested in my service in Vietnam. I still didn't like talking about it, but I gave him honest answers, and he seemed content with what I told him. At the end, he told me he was going to send my application to Headquarters in Washington D.C. for acceptance. I could not believe it. I didn't think he would do that. On other job interviews, all they said was, "We'll get back to you." But here he was flat out telling me that he was recommending me. I began to realize that this whole thing could actually happen.

I received my diploma from the University of Louisville in May. Nothing much changed after graduation. I continued in the same position at

GE. The whole thing seemed anticlimactic. I did have something to look forward to, however. I was anxiously waiting for some word from the FBI.

It turns out I didn't have long to wait. Two days after graduation I was working my shift, really focused on the work at hand. One of the assembly lines had gone down and we were trying to repair it. The longer it took, the farther overdue our production quota became. Getting behind wasn't the end of the world, but it wouldn't make my workers or me look good. I was elbow deep in the assembly line when my name was called over the intercom to report to the office for a phone call. I went and the secretary handed me the phone. It was a call from Western Union. The caller said she was going to read a telegram from J. Edgar Hoover. I practically fell to the floor. I don't remember the exact wording, but the message was that I had been accepted into the FBI as an agent, subject to completion of the training school in Washington D.C. and the FBI academy at Quantico Marine Base, Virginia. It was as simple as that. I don't know how I made it through the rest of my shift, but somehow I did.

I was over the moon. I called Ann and my father right away. My wife was supportive and happy, but she was also pregnant with our second child who was due to be born in February 1971. There was a lot going on in our lives but she was a trooper and behind me all the way.

I wasn't sure how my father would take the news. After how he responded to me being called to active duty, it could have gone any possible way. When I told him that I was going to be an FBI agent, he thought it was a joke. It took some talking, but I eventually convinced him this was legit. I could tell he was proud of me, but I think surprising him with the news took away some of his enthusiasm for this change in career.

In October 1970, almost exactly two years to the day from when I shipped off to Vietnam, I flew to Washington D.C. for training. My wife Ann stayed behind in anticipation of selling the house. I knew, as all the applicants did, we would be transferred to anywhere in the continental U. S. after completion of training, about four months away. She would have to be ready to move at the drop of a hat, not just now but from this point forward.

Leaving Ann behind with a toddler and a baby on the way wasn't fair to her. I knew that then and I know it now. I asked a lot of Ann, and she was willing to do what it took to support my career move. My son was due right at the end of my training. She would have to hold down the fort, care for our daughter, and deal with her pregnancy almost to the end all by herself. She sacrificed a lot in allowing me to follow this adventure. I'm grateful for her not standing in the way of all this, which she could have easily done.

The training was intense, fourteen weeks of academics, firearms training, physical fitness, and defensive tactics. The instructors even weighed us every day to make sure we were not over the acceptable limit. I don't know how we could have gained weight during that time, except maybe as muscle. This wasn't Fort Hood, but it wasn't a church social either. They put us through the ringer.

New Year 1971, right before graduation from the academy, we were told our city of assignment. Mine was Dallas, Texas, and I was very excited about this. I called Ann and told her the news.

She wasn't quite as enthusiastic, because it meant moving far from her family and support system, which she had needed often while I had been away. Now she would be on her own.

My fellow recruits and I were sent home to get our personal matters in order and given a time to report to our new office. Ann and I had to scramble to find a place to stay within a few weeks. We decided that Ann should stay behind until she had the baby, and then come across the country to Dallas to join me, with a toddler and baby in tow. I did everything I could to be supportive of Ann during this time. I wanted to do even more for her, but I didn't know what else could be done from halfway across the country. Soon enough, we were all in Dallas and I was off and running.

CHAPTER 6:
FIRST OFFICE AGENT

I had to report to Dallas in late January. I was nervous as I went into the office for the first time. That soon went away as the agents and staff were very welcoming. I was assigned to the Theft from Interstate Shipment (TFIS) squad. The Dallas area was a hub for shipment, which meant that there were literally thousands of semi-trucks coming through every day, and theft from interstate shipments was a federal crime. I was assigned a mentor who was to help me learn my job. Lamar Meyer was a very nice and more than capable agent. He took me on several of his cases and I sat in on some of his interviews. He had worked on the John F. Kennedy assassination and listening to him was fascinating. I was truly blessed to have him as my mentor.

I was at my desk one morning and Lamar said to come with him. We were going to the Dallas County Jail to conduct an interview. He drove to the jail and parked the car. We then walked down a ramp to get inside. I immediately recognized where I was. This was where Lee Harvey Oswald was shot by Jack Ruby. I knew this because I had watched this on television in Kentucky eight years before. Lamar asked, "Does this look familiar?" It sure did and it struck me, for the first time, that I was now a member of the world's elite law enforcement agency.

The interview at the jail was with an individual who had been arrested for carrying a gun on an airplane. Lamar was surprisingly very nice to the man. I asked Lamar about that, being nice, and he said, "Nothing wrong with being nice. I get more out of people being nice." I learned a huge lesson that day.

A few days later I was called to the main office and learned that Ann had had our second child.

The secretary booked me a flight to return to Kentucky to see my son. I visited for three days. It was an emotional time for me, considering how much time I had already spent away from my family. But at the end of my visit, I was ready to go back to Dallas. I was anxious to get back to work. My wife, daughter, and son would be arriving in Dallas soon, and when they did, we rented an apartment and began looking for a home to purchase.

I was enjoying my new career. Mostly my work up to now was reading cases and tagging along with agents on the squad. It was a good atmosphere, and I thrived in the environment. Tom Carpenter was right, I was meant to be an FBI agent.

One day, I was sitting at my desk and the supervisor handed me a new case that had just been reported. I was thrilled. I was a "first office" agent, as we were called, a newcomer, and was watched carefully and usually did not get assigned cases for some time. First office agents as a rule were never assigned high profile cases. The veteran agents did not want anyone to ruin their career by doing something stupid; all us newbies had better be on our good behavior and not embarrass the office or the organization.

I reviewed the case as much as I could as there was not a great deal of information. I was anxious to get out of the office, get in an FBI car, and go to the scene. The case was a theft of goods from a semi-truck, which was a federal violation. I did not yet know what the truck was carrying. I arrived at the loading dock and met the manager. He told me the driver had reported a theft from his truck and it must have occurred at a drop off from a previous delivery. I looked in the truck and it was filled with toilet paper! What a load, no pun intended! I followed the investigative rule learned at the training academy, interviewed the driver, contacted the shipper, then typed up and filed my report. As it turned out the dollar amount of the theft did not reach the threshold required for investigation. The case of the missing toilet paper was closed.

It was not long after that I was riding with Lamar Meyer going to an interview. We received a radio call from the SAC of the Dallas office. He told me to report to him. Was I scared or was I scared? I had no idea what was going on. Lamar tried to calm me, but it was too late, I was in a panic. We arrived at the building. I went to the main office and waited for the SAC to call me in. I walked in and my supervisor was sitting there. I could not figure out what I may have done. I was told to sit down and the SAC asked, "How would you like to go to the Amarillo office?" I could hardly catch my breath. The Amarillo, Texas, FBI office was one of several Resident Agencies (RA) in the Dallas territory. First office agents usually were not assigned to a small office for several reasons, mainly lack of experience and little or no opportunity for supervision. In an RA you work any and all types of cases and violations rather than be pigeon-holed working one or a few federal violations. I was thrilled to be given this opportunity. I like to think it was due to my experience with management at GE and leadership in the military where I learned to be a team player and be willing to take on any task, no matter how small. I must have done something right, at any rate, because it was very early in my career to be sent to an RA.

Ann and I had been looking for a house to buy in Dallas while living in an apartment with a month to month lease. Ann was not very happy about moving to Amarillo, but it wasn't quite as traumatic as moving from Kentucky to Dallas. She hadn't put down roots yet, and the children were far too young to be settled in a school that we wouldn't want to take them away from. So we packed up our apartment in Dallas and drove to Amarillo. We arrived and got a hotel. I went to the FBI office the next morning and met the all the agents there. Everyone was great and welcomed me. I was allowed a week to find a place to live for my family. We made a good profit from the house we sold in Kentucky, allowing us to find a very nice house in Amarillo. The home we found was under construction and would be completed within the month. The hotel was very nice to give us a good rate and even an adjoining room for our toddler daughter and infant son.

We finally were able to move into the house. I was working a lot of cases, and I was having the time of my life. Everyone in the office got along well and they accepted me with open arms. I was willing to do anything, go anywhere, and help anyone. I earned respect for my work ethic and friendship. I worked bank robberies, interstate car thefts, check frauds, fugitive cases, and anything else that was needed. I gained confidence every day.

I remember a case I was working then. I was investigating a fraudulent check case in which an individual was cashing checks between banks in Oklahoma and Texas. This guy was slick, and I was having difficulty gathering much evidence. I was able to get a license number from a bank teller who suspected something and jotted down the plate. Not long after, I was working with an agent from the office on one of his cases. He was driving towards the office on Route 66. When we stopped at a traffic light, I looked over to my right and there was a car that matched what witnesses had identified as the car the check writer was driving, a Cadillac. The car was in the right lane and stopped at the traffic light. I asked the agent driving to get behind the Cadillac as I wanted to see the license plate. The agent was not very happy. I knew he wanted to go home for the day. He was probably thinking, "This kid had better be right."

We got behind the car and the plate matched. A male was driving, and there was a female passenger. I said to the agent I wanted to pull the car over to check identification. I spoke to the driver and he had the same name that had been mentioned in the case. I did not have a warrant with me for his arrest, so I asked the driver if he would follow us to the sheriff's office for questioning. He got in his car and we both pulled out onto the highway. The agent driving radioed the sheriff's office and asked for identification of the car and the person driving. Within three minutes, there was feedback from surrounding counties in Texas and Oklahoma telling us the individual was wanted. He had 17 warrants out for his arrest.

I don't know what made the suspect follow us, but he was still behind us after we heard the radio traffic, and we were afraid he might run for it. We arrived at the county jail and told him he was wanted and took him into the jail. Because we did not have a warrant, he was turned over to the local authorities. We drove to the FBI office, and as we did the agent, a veteran, turned to me and said, "That was good work." A couple of weeks passed, and the agent came to my desk with a Letter of Commendation from J. Edgar Hoover for identifying the person and being responsible for bringing him to justice. I was shocked that I had a letter from the Director of the FBI. To this day I am grateful for being recognized, as I was told there was not many first office agents who received such an honor.

CHAPTER 7:
HARRISBURG, PENNSYLVANIA

Even though I had been transferred to Amarillo soon after starting in Dallas, I was still considered a first office agent. All first office agents were transferred to what was called their "duty office" after one year. That assignment was generally for three to five years. My first year was coming to a close, and Ann and I had to start thinking about moving again.

Ann and I loved the house we had found in Amarillo. The children were happy there, and the house had a fence around our big backyard which allowed them to play without being in danger from the nearby road. Ann had found a church and we attended almost every Sunday. Even though we really liked the people, I did find some of them a bit off-putting. I had been attending Sunday bible study with Ann. One day another one of the attendees started lecturing everyone on how much money we should be giving to the church. I felt that he was out of line, and I never went back to that bible study class. That didn't do much for our social life, because we didn't have many friends in Amarillo, and most of our friends came from the church. It's hard to make friends in one year.

I really liked Amarillo. It had been a great learning experience. The fellow agents had been friendly and helpful in getting me through my first year, including me in their investigations, interviews, and arrests. But I knew we were not going to be staying in Texas.

For some reason, in the Amarillo area, there were quite a few bad check cases. I guess because it is situated in the panhandle of Texas there is easy access to several states nearby. Crossing state lines to commit a crime brought it under federal jurisdiction most of the time. Another type of case we saw often was interstate transportation of a stolen motor vehicle. Between checks and stolen cars, I was kept very busy.

At one point I was assigned a case that originated out of Oklahoma. Bad checks were being cashed in Oklahoma, New Mexico, and Texas. The banks in Amarillo had been hit several times, and little or no evidence was available. There were no photos, no fingerprints, no license plate numbers to track down or investigate. No one could get an ID on the person writing the bad checks. The only thing we had was that the check-passer was a very large woman.

The Oklahoma office finally got a lead, and discovered she was living in Amarillo. The Oklahoma office had enough evidence to arrest her and obtained a warrant. The agent working the case in Oklahoma sent a teletype to me which said "locate and apprehend." I went to the residence, but no one was home. I talked to the neighbors, but no one wanted to talk or simply said "I don't know anything." I made several visits but could not find anyone there. I took a chance by going back to one of the neighbors I had previously interviewed and talking to him. I told him I had a warrant for her arrest and asked him if he had seen her go in or out of the house. He said, "Why don't you come here at night?" I thanked him. It was reasonably clear that he wanted to help but didn't want to get involved. That was fine by me.

I returned to my office and asked agent Larry Steging if he would assist me with the arrest. Later that evening Larry drove me to the residence. There was a light on, so I knocked loudly on the door and announced that it was the FBI and I had a warrant. If they didn't open the door, I would kick it in. We could hear people walking around and then the door opened. I asked the woman who answered for her name, and it was the same person wanted by the Oklahoma office. I took her to the car without handcuffs because her wrists were so large I couldn't get the bracelets to go around them. I put her in the backseat of the car and sat next to her, ordering her to keep her hands where I could see them. Larry drove us to the Potter County jail in Amarillo. It was a very hot evening. The temperature was in the 90s and the jail did not have air conditioning. We got her out of the car and took her to the third floor. Larry said he would fingerprint her while I interviewed her to complete the identification. Larry and I both wore suits and all of us were sweating, including her. I could see something was wrong, but it was too late. She turned and threw up on Larry. It was so disgusting that it was all I could do not to throw up myself. Some of the jail personnel came and put her in a cell. I felt badly for Larry, considering it was my case and he was only helping me.

Finally, my transfer from Amarillo came in. I received my order to report to Philadelphia within thirty days. My wife and I began preparations for the move. Right after that, I received a call from agent Mike Wald who worked with Tom Carpenter in the Louisville office. Mike had been transferred to the Harrisburg, Pennsylvania Resident Agency, which had its headquarters in Philadelphia. He asked if I would be interested in coming to Harrisburg as there was a vacancy there. Naturally, I said yes. FBI headquarters in Washington changed my orders to Harrisburg. I was elated.

The movers picked up our furniture and we made the long trek to Pennsylvania. We put our stuff in storage in Harrisburg until we could find a place to live. After staying in a hotel for two or three weeks, we found a house in a nice area with good schools in Mechanicsburg. We moved in and I went to work. I was eager to learn this new office and the cases I would have there. Mike Wald and I became partners and good friends during that time. Sadly, he died several years ago. I was lucky to spend ten years in Harrisburg and was able to work several high profile cases, including the Mainline Murder, which is what we called the murder of Susan Reinert and the kidnapping of her two children (more on that in Chapter 8).

I have to admit that socializing wasn't my top priority. I was working all the time; nights, weekends, whenever I was needed. I was getting comfortable with the office, my cases, and my friendships with the other agents. I can't say enough about how great it was to work with the local law agencies. Many of the friends I did have came from the local police, sheriffs, and state troopers who were always willing to help the FBI.

In my time in Harrisburg, I worked so many cases I couldn't count them all. A few stand out, however. For example, one time this one guy whose name escapes me robbed a bank using a gun. He wasn't terribly successful, only getting out of the bank with a few thousand dollars. He got away from the bank, but not from me. He was a junkie who was fixing a couple of times a day, and I was able to track him down through some information gained from informants we were working with. We are not magicians and to meet and greet the people who were the source of drugs, an informant was often necessary. After we arrested robber, we took him to be arraigned and he plead not guilty. In the courthouse there was an FBI office and a U.S. Marshal's office. The Marshals had a holding area, so we kept him there for a while. I was in the FBI office in the courthouse when the Marshal called me up to tell me that the bank robber wanted to talk to me. I went up to visit him in his cell. I looked him over, and he looked like he was in terrible shape. He was one of the worst junkies I'd ever met. He must have been six foot two inches and couldn't have weighed more than 130 pounds. He must have been missing his next fix because he was ready to make a deal.

I said, "What's up? What do you want?"

He looked at me and said, "I'm not saying I did it, but would it help if I showed you where the money is?"

I almost laughed. It would certainly help me, but not so much him or his case. But of course I didn't tell him that. I just said what I said to every suspect who wanted to cut a deal. I told him that I couldn't promise him anything, but I would see what I could do. I went back down to the office and told Mike Wald that the guy wanted to show us where the money was. A local detective, Bob Warner, who had helped work the case was there at the same time. We considered the offer, which was an unusual one. We didn't usually have the opportunity retrieve the money. It was usually spent or lost. In this case, it was only a few thousand dollars, hardly important except for its evidentiary value. We talked it over and decided it was worth a try.

Detective Warner, Mike Wald, and I went back to the Marshal's office and collected the junkie to go find the money. We put him in cuffs behind his back and took him down to my car.

I had a new government car. This was the first *new* car I had ever been issued. Most of the time the cars they provided us were in terrible shape, hand-me-downs at best, junkers at worst. This car still had that "new car" smell to it. I was very proud of it.

I drove. Detective Warner was in the back with the junkie, and Mike Wald was in the front with me. We had been driving for over an hour to some very rural area of Cumberland County, Pennsylvania. Along the way, the junkie announced he was going to throw up. Even though I was driving, I turned to look at him and said, "If you throw up in my car, you are going to be in big trouble!" Apparently, he was serious about his condition because he began to turn green. I pulled off to the side of the road and he threw up outside of my car. But it was very close.

After we got him back in the car, he started giving directions again. We came to a dirt road, and he instructed me to turn left. We took that road for about a half mile, and as we approached a very steep hill that was on the side of the road, he told me to stop. We got him out of the car, and Mike and I grabbed him and said, "Now what?" He said the money was buried at the top, so we began to climb.

When I say this was a steep hill, I mean it was practically vertical. Mike and I were carrying shovels and dragging this junkie up the hill with us, but it was very slow going because he had his hands cuffed behind him. We stopped and I switched the cuffs so that he had his hands in front and could pull himself up the hill using his hands. At the crest of the hill, he told us to stop and pointed to an area of the ground. "Right there." We sat him on a tree stump and started digging. We dug all over that area but didn't find anything. I turned to him to ask him what the deal was. As I turned, I saw this guy, who was unnaturally skinny, pull his hands from the cuffs. He took off. I saw him do this, but Mike didn't. I yelled to Mike to follow and began running after the junkie. Mike was already far behind because he had a bad start. I have to tell you, as I was running after that guy, all I could think was there goes my career. An agent simply did not allow a suspect to escape him after he was in custody. Yet there went my suspect, running at full tilt, taking my career with him.

The junkie must have been getting tired because I began gaining on him. He reached a dip in the hill and disappeared. I was only a few steps behind, and I saw that he hadn't run away, he had slipped and hit his head on something, cutting it open and bleeding everywhere. I caught up to him and cuffed him again. Boy, was I mad. I hauled him to his feet and started marching him, bleeding terribly, back to the car. I quickly met Bob Warner because he had been tracing our progress from the bottom of the hill. I shoved the junkie at Bob and said, "Here. He's yours." Bob got him back to the car and wrapped a towel around his head. If there was an emergency room anywhere in Cumberland County, I wouldn't know it. I took him back to Harrisburg, over an hour away, listening to him moan and complain about his head the whole time.

We got him into the ER in Harrisburg, and I'll tell you, we kept our hands on him the whole time. They took him right away. The doctor there told us that he needed stiches. I couldn't believe it, but this fool refused treatment. He would not allow the doctor to stitch him up. I told the guy if he didn't get stitched up, we were taking him back to lockup. Before we could leave, another, more senior doctor came in and started accusing us of having beaten the junkie up. I told the doctors, either treat him or we're taking him with us, but we didn't beat him up. The junkie still refused treatment. The doctors put some butterfly bandages on his cut, and we took him back to the Marshal's lockup. As we pushed him into the cell, he turned to me and said, "Where do you want to go next time, Redden?" What a jerk.

As we were leaving the, one of the Marshals stopped us. He said, "I need to tell you something. Before you left, I heard your suspect on the phone with someone. He insisted on making a call and took a few tries to get whoever it was on the phone. I heard something that might have been him planning with someone else to ambush you out in the woods." I was grateful to the Marshal for telling me, but I really wish he had said something before we left.

The junkie was ultimately convicted of the bank robbery, but it didn't end there. The whole office knew I had almost lost my suspect. In the Harrisburg office we had a monthly award for the agent who screwed up the most. The award was called the Julius Mingroni award. Julius Mingroni was an osteopathic doctor who was the center of a scandal involving payoffs to some senator to not only get Julius into osteopath school, but make sure he graduated. Julius had an IQ of about 80. That month, I received the Julius Mingroni award. It was a ceramic gnome with a missing leg and a chipped little pointy hat. It looked like it had been dug out of a landfill. I had the privilege of keeping that little ugly thing on my desk the whole month through.

There were many bank robberies in Harrisburg during my time there. I remember there were 32 robberies, and we solved 31 of them. One was particularly quick to be solved. This young man went into a bank to rob it. He was wearing very tight blue jeans. He asked for the money, and the teller did her job and gave him the money, but also gave him a dye pack. The robber shoved the money into his pants, in his crotch area. He wouldn't have done that if he knew he had that dye pack. They are set to explode when you leave the door of the bank. That's what happened to this poor bank robber. The dye pack went off, and he ran down the street, teargas and smoke streaming from his crotch. A local police officer saw him and picked him up. The robber was lucky he didn't blow his balls off!

Later, another bank got hit. There were no cameras, no metal detectors, no security of any significance. Needless to say, it was held up often. This one time, three armed guys ran into the bank wearing masks, and they robbed the bank. They got out and ran to their car, which was a block away. They left no evidence to be found. Not so much as a fingerprint. We did a neighborhood search for the car, hoping someone saw it or the three guys. At one place, an elderly black woman came to the door. She wouldn't open it, but just shouted to the agent. He asked if she saw anything worth reporting. As it turned out, she had. The day of the robbery, she saw three guys jump into a Cadillac with a pink shag rug on the trunk lid. That's all she knew, but it turned out that was enough. We went back to the bank and the manager gave us a list of the serial numbers from the stolen money. While we were there, other agents were cordoning off the city, leaving no exits without an agent there watching. We went through the streets looking for the Cadillac. I spotted the car parked on the street. That woman had not been kidding. It was a Cadillac with a pink shag carpet on the trunk. We radioed for backup and surveillance. One hour later, sure enough, three guys came out of a house, got into the Cadillac, and drove off. We followed them to the nearest Kentucky Fried Chicken, and they went inside. A few minutes later, they came out with a big bucket of chicken. Some of our agents followed them while I went inside to talk to the manager. I asked him, "How did those three guys pay for their meal?" The manager reached into the cash drawer and pulled out a $20, holding it with two fingers like it was a loaded diaper. We checked the list of stolen bills, and what do you know? The twenty was on the bait list. We almost didn't catch them but for an unlikely tip on a pink shag rug and a $20 bill. Nevertheless, the suspects didn't do anything to try to keep themselves anonymous. A pink shag rug? Really?

In another case, two young kids robbed a bank at gunpoint. One of the robbers kicked an old woman in the stomach. Fortunately, she was okay, but it didn't do anything to kindly dispose us to these guys. We had an ID on the car they used, and the State Police found it quickly. I drove down to Carlisle, Pennsylvania to arrest them. One of them confessed right away, then the other one broke down. It turned out that they had been back in the woods smoking weed, and they ran out of both drugs and money. So they thought, "Why don't we rob a bank?" These were kids barely out of high school. One of them even had a football scholarship to college. Neither one had ever been in trouble before. Of course, we had to lock them up. I went to see their parents, and I was sick at heart for having to break the news to them that their sons would be going to prison. At one of their houses, the father was there, and he let another agent and me in. Before I could explain why I was there, the mother came into the living room. The father said, "These gentlemen are here from the FBI. It's something to do with [their son]." When I explained what he had done, his mother started crying. I really felt for those parents. That boy was convicted and served five years in prison. He threw his life away. It really was a shame.

Then there was a time when an inmate was released from Louisburg Federal Prison in Pennsylvania. He was released at 10 AM. They put him on a bus, and he went to Harrisburg, arriving around noon. Those prisons don't exactly give released inmates a wad of cash to get them started in a new life. He was broke. What else could he do but rob a bank? He didn't do any preparation and had no idea of how to get away. At 1 PM he went into a bank and robbed it. As he was trying to escape, he made a wrong turn and went down a corridor with no outlet. There happened to be a local policeman in the bank at the time, and he locked down the building. The robber was quickly caught. By 2 PM, he was on a bus back to the prison because he had violated the terms of his release. As he was boarding, I was standing next to him. I asked him, "How was your vacation, pal?"

We used informants extensively in FBI work. There was one bank robbery where the suspect got away with a great deal of money. We had no leads, but when one criminal was busted for drugs, he was willing to talk. I asked him, "Who robbed the bank?" He gave me the name of Daryl Dorsey. It turned out that the informant was close to Dorsey's girlfriend. We didn't have a line on Dorsey's whereabouts, so we had to wait for a break. It came a few days later when the informant called. It turned out that the girlfriend was going to be getting on a train to Philadelphia to visit Dorsey. We hightailed it to the train station. Another agent and I got on the same train as her, separately so she wouldn't realize we were together. When we got to Philadelphia, the local police were waiting for us, as was another FBI agent, who was at the door of the train car. When the girlfriend stood up, the other agent and I got up as well. She stepped off the train and was spotted by the local FBI agent, and we all followed he. As I was getting off the train, some of the other agents identified Dorsey as he was standing at the ticket desk. When approached by the agents, Dorsey gave himself up.

There was also a great deal of theft at the local railroad yard. It was the largest railroad yard on the East Coast, with hundreds of trains stopping there every day. Naturally, it was a target for theft, considering all the valuable stuff that was being shipped and loaded there. I spent several years investigating thefts from that railroad yard under the Theft from Interstate Shipment laws, just like back in Amarillo.

One time, I was on surveillance with another agent. We spotted two guys who had come to rob a train. We approached them as they were in the act of robbing a train car, but we were spotted and the subjects ran. There were two of them and two of us. They split up, and I took one while my partner took the other. My suspect was able to run at top speed, but I wasn't. I was weighed down with radios, guns, etc. The subject got to a tall fence and went right over, but I wasn't able to. I had to look for another way to get through the fence. Fortunately, I found one. There was my guy, running too far ahead for me to reach him. I figured, well, I'll catch him eventually. As I watched, he jumped in a car, which I figured was his getaway vehicle. I was far away from my vehicle, so I couldn't chase him. But then they started up, made a U-turn, and came towards me. I jumped out into the middle of the street and waved my hands. "Stop, stop!" I shouted. Surprisingly, the car stopped. The driver rolled down his window and called to me. "Redden? Is that you?" The driver turned out to be a detective I knew from the local police department who had been on a stakeout of his own, nothing to do with mine. His name was Detective Henry Heisey. I said, "Hey, Henry." Henry asked, "Are you looking for this guy?" I said, "Yes, sir, I am." My suspect had jumped into the back of the car, but because it was a police car there was no way to get out without one of us letting him out. He was stuck. I don't know if he was relieved or not when I pulled him out , but he wasn't getting away again. All he had to say for himself was "Shoot!"

Every Sunday, a train loaded with meat would arrive in Harrisburg. They always stopped there and changed crews before continuing on to their final destination. Within 15 minutes, thieves would show up, and it was like a feeding frenzy. They would just go in and take what they wanted, sometimes entire sides of beef. Although we knew that the were there, we had the worst time catching them. One time, I was on one side of the car and another agent was on the other, with the thieves in the middle. Somehow we got our signals crossed and the thieves were alerted to our presence. They ran, taking the meat with them. The trainyard was very dusty and dirty, with standing water everywhere. Of course, the thief dropped the side of beef in some of the dirty water, ruining it. When the thieves did get away with the meat, they would sell it to local restaurants. One restaurant in particular bought a lot of it, which was much less expensive than wholesale. I brought the owner into the office one time for questioning, and he denied buying it. I threatened to bring in the Department of Health to do an inspection. That was enough for the owner. He admitted buying the stolen meat, which was receiving stolen goods, a felony. I didn't charge him because he cooperated. He gave up the thieves, and I finally caught them.

There were other kinds of crimes we worked as well. For example, I worked a horse rustling ring case. There's a particular breed of horse named Tennessee Walkers. They walk with a very exaggerated step, and if you ever saw one, you wouldn't forget it. There was a big controversy between Kentucky and Tennessee over these horses, especially when some were stolen. There was a man I knew in southern Pennsylvania, which was my territory, who was testifying for the federal government in a case in Tennessee about the stolen horses. When certain people found out this man was testifying, he started getting death threats. We knew each other, and he called me for help. I worked it out so that another agent and I were able to go stay at his farm in Hannover, Pennsylvania. We were there for a weekend, and truth be told, we had a marvelous time. He had a big family, and we played basketball with his kids, and played softball with the whole family. I happen to be a horse enthusiast, and I saw that this man had some of the Tennessee Walkers, similar to the ones he was testifying about. I had never ridden one before. He offered to let me ride. When the weekend was over, he drove himself to Tennessee. Later on, I learned that the horses we had ridden were some of the stolen ones. If I had known that, I certainly wouldn't have been riding them. I would have arrested that man right then and there.

One weekend, I was the duty agent on call. One of the detectives in Carlisle, Pennsylvania had a farm where he raised chickens. Every year he would slaughter the chickens. It was a lot of work. He called me and asked if I wanted some of the chickens. They were very good eating, so of course I was interested. He wanted me to come down and help slaughter the chickens, and then he would give me some to take home. When I arrived at his farm, it was clear that the detective had called some other people for help, because there were several others there. If you've never slaughtered a chicken before, be advised that it is not a neat process. There's a lot of blood everywhere, and by the end of the first hour, I was covered in chicken blood. That's when a local police vehicle arrived. The officer stepped out and called, "Is there an Agent Redden here?" I answered in the affirmative. It turned out that there was a man threatening to blow up a motel nearby, and because I was the duty agent, it was my responsibility to go to the scene. I looked at myself, and I was a bloody mess. I shouldn't go to a crime scene like that, but I didn't have any choice. There was no time to go home and put on clean clothes. The police officer drove me to the motel, and I stepped out of the car to be greeted by a dozen police officers and the local news. I cannot emphasize enough how awful I looked, like I had just come from a murder scene, and I was the murderer. But it was my duty to find out what was going on and take care of it. I went up to the police commander and asked what I could do for him. Evidently the suspect in the motel wanted to talk to an FBI agent. I looked over at the TV cameras, and really didn't want to be seen covered in blood. But the commander asked if I would please go talk to the guy. I had no idea if I was going to get in trouble for looking so awful when technically I was on duty. I was scared, too. I didn't have any body armor, and I wasn't armed. But I went to the motel room door and knocked. I called out, "FBI! Come to the door!" The suspect came to the door. He was probably in his sixties or seventies, and something was definitely wrong with him. He asked, "Who do you work for?" I told him I was an FBI agent. "Who is the director of the FBI?" he asked. I didn't answer, but said, "Can you please come out? Is there something we can help you with?" It turned out that the man just wanted to talk to the FBI, if for no other reason than to do it. He was a kook. I went back to the police commander and let him take over. They wound up shooting tear gas into the window. When they pulled the suspect out of the hotel room, we learned that he had wired the door to explode. Fortunately, he didn't have any actual explosives, but the door was indeed "wired" to "explode" when opened. We were lucky that time.

I also had more than my fair share of problems on airplanes. One time, Mike Wald and I were on a plane traveling to Pittsburgh. We were armed, which mean that we had to report to the pilot and announce ourselves. On a plane, even though we are federal agents, the captain is totally in charge. We took our seats, with Mike one row ahead of me. During the flight, a man began tugging on the skirt of one of the attendants. She tried to distance herself from him, but he kept pulling on her skirt. Mike and I saw this, but we didn't react. It wasn't our place to intervene, since being a jerk wasn't exactly a federal crime. As we approached Pittsburgh and began our descent, this same man got out of his seat, went up to the cockpit, and started looking at the passengers like he wanted to say or do something. Of course, an attendant asked him to take his seat, but he refused. Another attendant came to me for help, and I said I would be able to help if I had permission from the pilot. By this time, the copilot had come out of the cockpit, and the individual had started yelling. The copilot came down the aisle and asked Mike and me for help. That was all we needed. I went up to the front and quietly asked the man to sit down. The flight rules were that we couldn't land with this idiot out of his seat; he would be delaying everyone by standing. I told him Mike and I had a meeting to go to, and all these other nice people had places to be. I asked him again to sit, but he simply said, "Go fuck yourself." That was good enough for me. I grabbed him and took him to the floor. I had no cuffs, so I asked a pair of people in first class to find other seats. Mike and I sat him down right there, and I sat next to him. I turned to the man and said, "What is wrong with you?" He actually said, "I'm really sorry." "Well, it's much too late for that." I had the pilot call the Pittsburgh police, and they were ready for us when we arrived. Two big cops were waiting on the tarmac for us. Everyone on the plane applauded me as I pushed him out the door. Interfering with flight operations is simply a misdemeanor, but the guy didn't need to know that. I was perfectly content with the police taking him away with him thinking he was going to prison. About thirty days later, I was on the same flight, and it turned out that one of the attendants had also been on the previous trip. She saw me and recognized me right away.

She seemed very happy to see me. I went back to my seat, and discovered there were a pair of U.S. Marshals transporting some prisoners on that flight. I struck up a conversation with them, but was soon interrupted by the attendant from the earlier flight. She said, "I never had a chance to thank you," and gave me a big hug. This embarrassed me, especially in front of the Marshals, who were laughing at me. But she was very easy on the eyes, and I returned the hug. The rest of the flight, that attendant made sure I had whatever I wanted. It was a good flight.

These were just a few of the stand-out cases and incidents during my time in Harrisburg.

CHAPTER 8:
THE MAINLINE MURDERS:
SUSAN REINERT
AND HER MISSING CHILDREN,
1979

It had been almost ten years in Harrisburg. I had some good cases during that time and was enjoying my career. Looking back now, it's clear I made the right decision to join the FBI. GE had given me a good start, and I learned a lot from them that helped me succeed in the Bureau. Things were going my way. I was very goal oriented and solving each case was my number one priority. I was willing to take calculated risks in order to succeed. I was not swayed by negative or positive feedback as I knew both were essential in order to gain respect.

One day in June 1979, as I was reading the newspaper at my desk, I noticed an article regarding the death of a woman. She had been found nude in the hatchback trunk of a car, which later turned out to be her own. The car was found in the parking lot of a hotel in Swarara Township, a few miles from Harrisburg in Dauphin County, Pennsylvania. As I read on, I saw the Pennsylvania State Police was working the case along with the local authorities. The chief investigating officer with the State Police was Jack Holtz, whom I knew well. We had worked several cases together and were friends. I telephoned Jack. I told him I had read the article and offered the FBI's help with any out of state leads, if he needed it. Jack was a competent veteran with the State Police. He told me the victim was Susan Reinert, a high school teacher from the Philadelphia area, and she had two children who were still missing. There really wasn't anything he needed me to do then, but he was thankful for my offer.

A couple of weeks passed, and I did not hear anything from Jack. Not long after, I received a call from Ken Reinert, the victim's estranged husband. I told him I knew of his wife's murder. Reinert was frantic to find his children and asked if the FBI could get involved as he did not believe enough progress was being made by the local or state police. I explained to him that the state police were very capable and for the FBI to get involved we would need them to request our assistance. Only then we could help investigate. This was not the answer he was looking for and he implored me to take over, but I told him that I couldn't. Not long after this, a congressman requested the FBI get involved as thirty days had passed with no known result from the investigation and no sign of the children.

Evidently the congressman, Ken Reinert, or both had called FBI headquarters and managed to find someone there who was prepared to break protocol. HQ ordered us to become involved in this case and help the state police find the missing children, Karen and Michael, ages eleven and ten. The supervisor of the Harrisburg office appointed me case agent in charge of the investigation for the FBI. I was happy with this turn of events. I immediately contacted the state police to set up a meeting at their headquarters. That's when things became challenging.

Jack Holtz and Joe Van Nort briefed us on the evidence and their progress The investigation was taking place in the Philadelphia area even though the case began in Harrisburg. Holtz and I had a good working relationship, but I knew Van Nort could be trouble. He was a veteran with the state police and did not like the FBI. He thought we were going to take the case from him. Even when I told him we were there to help find the children and the case belonged to the state police, he was still openly hostile. Joe was considerably older than the rest of us, stuck in his ways, and distrustful of anyone horning in on his territory. I got the impression that he wanted credit for solving the case to further his career. That was fine by me. All I was interested in was locating the children. Joe could take credit for that too, if he wanted it.

Nothing I did could convince Joe we weren't there to cause trouble. This was a very important case and he wanted all the glory. He was ornery, quite frankly, and I sparred with him frequently. He would argue with me daily and I never could convince him that we were here to help despite how many times I reminded him this was a state police case. He would complain unnecessarily about our agents, men and women I knew well. His concerns were ridiculous, and completely off base. He made it clear that he hated me, our agents, and our presence in *his* investigation. All of this was internal and did not interfere with the job of investigating the murder of Susan or searching for her two children. We all wanted the same results.

It was a lost cause with Joe, and unfortunately I never had a chance to make it right with him. Around that time, Joe took a day off to travel back to Harrisburg to qualify for firearms training. As he was shooting on the range, he suffered a heart attack and died.

It was agreed we would use the Belmont State Police building as our headquarters. This choice was less than convenient for all of us, because Belmont was two and a half hours west of Harrisburg, and even farther from Philadelphia, which was four hours east. But we made it work.

When we were all together, the State Police briefed me and my agents on the case. During the initial stages of the case there were eighteen FBI agents and an equal number of State Police officers. We matched an agent and trooper together to conduct the necessary interviews.

Susan Reinert was last seen on June 22, 1979 just after dark driving away from her home with her children in the car, the same vehicle she was found in three days later. On June 25, early in the day, her nude body was found lying in the fetal position in the cargo area of her car, with the hatchback open. The car had been observed with the trunk open as early as the night before. She had been chained, beaten, strangled, and asphyxiated. She had extensive bleeding in the area of one eye, and bruises on her back were consistent with the imprint of a chain. The actual cause of death was asphyxiation from an overdose of morphine, "which was consistent with having been caused by a criminal agency," according to the coroner.

We learned from the briefing that two individuals, Dr. Jay C. Smith and William Bradfield, were named as persons of interest in the death of Susan Reinert. Smith was the principal of Upper Merion High School and Bradfield was an English teacher at the same school, where Susan Reinert was also a teacher. Despite being a month into the investigation, there were still hundreds of interviews that needed to be done.

Mike Wald and I would drive to Belmont, stay in a motel for the week, and return home on Friday. As agents and state police officers conducted interviews, they would report back to us for further instructions based on the results. We interviewed teachers, parents, neighbors, friends, and anyone that may help in finding the children. Since more than a month had passed, we all believed Karen and Michael were dead. That didn't stop us from looking for them.

Something else was wrong. No one wanted to talk to us. The resistance we received from nearly everyone was astonishing. Most disturbing were the teachers at the school. Everyone seemed to be either afraid or actually supportive of Bradfield. He had a circle of friends, mostly young female teachers who seemed to worship him.

I was the case agent for the FBI, so I was primarily in the command post at the State Police

Barracks, reviewing results of interviews, trying to make sense of this complex case. I was able to conduct a few interviews myself and could not believe the response from the teachers at Upper Merion High School. They did not want to answer questions about the murder. During one interview, I was getting agitated with a teacher and said, "Do you know we are trying to find two young children?" I was angry they were unwilling to help.

Bradfield was, for a lack of better terms, a lowlife conman. He had convinced Susan to withdraw $25,000 from her savings account for him to invest, but it was all bogus. He gave the money to Wendy Ziegler, who was also smitten with Bradfield and was one of his many affairs, to put in a safe deposit box. Wendy was arrested as an accomplice in that case of fraud. The police investigators convinced her to testify against Bradfield in exchange for her charges being dismissed. While Bradfield was in jail, waiting for the fraud trial, he had her retrieve the $25,000. To make matters more bizarre, Bradfield filed suit to try to claim the $730,000 from Susan's life insurance policy. Bradfield was convicted of the fraud and was sentenced to two years.

William Bradfield was having an affair with Susan Reinert, and had been since 1973, when her children were 4 and 5 years old, respectively. We had reason to believe that the affair with Bradfield was a contributing factor to the breakup of her marriage, but since it wasn't directly related to the case, we didn't pursue that line. As we conducted our interviews, it became clear that Susan was smitten with Bradfield and wanted to be married to him in the worst way, and that he had promised to marry Susan in the summer, approximately the same time as the murder. We learned Susan had changed her will to make him the primary beneficiary instead of her brother. Even the children were omitted and would not receive anything. Susan had also made Bradfield the sole beneficiary on a life insurance policy for $730,000 she had taken out just thirty days before she was found murdered. She. On the policy, she wrote, "William Bradfield, my future husband." She also made him the guardian of her children in the event of her death.

Another complicating factor was that Bradfield was living with a woman named Susan Meyers, known as Sue. Susan Reinert tolerated

Sue Meyers' presence in Bradfield's life, but her attachment to Bradfield was such that she allowed him to come to her house whenever he wanted sex. Bradfield had been keeping his promises of marriage secret from his friends, and had told Sue Meyers that he wasn't interested in Susan even though she was enamored with him. On one occasion, Susan Reinert and Sue Meyers got into a fight over Bradfield at school. It was mostly shouting, no physical contact, but from what we were able to learn it was a nasty fight. The irony was that neither one of them knew he was having affairs with not only the two of them, but several women, including two other teachers and a former student.

Sue Meyers refused to talk at all. We obtained a subpoena for her to appear before the Grand Jury that was empaneled for this case. A State Trooper and I went to serve the subpoena. I knocked and she opened the door as far as the chain would go. I ask if she wanted to talk and she said no. I handed her the subpoena through the door, telling her she had to report to the Grand Jury. She tried to slam the door on my hand, but the State Trooper stopped her. It was a good thing he had fast reflexes, because I could have lost a finger or two to the closing door.

The other suspect, Dr. Jay C. Smith, the principal of the high school, was strange to say the least. When I say that the teachers were unwilling to talk, I meant about Bradfield. They were more than happy to spout rumors and speculation about Smith. There were so many stories about him, it was mind boggling. Sex parties with teachers, pornography, devil worship, and body parts buried on the school grounds. His daughter and son-in-law, both heroin addicts, were missing and presumed dead. Dr. Smith had previously been arrested at St. David's Mall in Montgomery County, Pennsylvania for theft. The police had found drugs, guns, and burglary tools in Smith's car. They searched his home and found pornography—mostly bestiality stuff, nitric acid which can be used to drug or kill, security guard uniforms, and badges. They linked Smith to two Sears store thefts. He was brought up on robbery charges. For this case, when Smith went to trial Bradfield was the alibi witness. The jury did not buy it and convicted Smith of all charges. He was let out of jail until sentencing.

There were well over a hundred interviews conducted in the Reinert case with little results due to the reluctance of many of our potential witnesses. There was also little physical evidence. There was a comb found underneath Susan's body with the letters 79 USARCOM. This was a military designation and possible evidence leading to Smith as he was a Colonel in that unit in the Army Reserves. Additionally, a green pin with the letter "P" in white was found in Smith's car. The pin was a souvenir from the Philadelphia Museum of Art where Karen and her classmates had recently toured. Susan's neighbors had observed Karen wearing the pin when Susan left in her car with her children the last time anyone saw them. There was also a tape of a call made to the local police department. The caller said there was a body in the trunk of a car in the parking lot of a motel and it was open. That recording was destroyed by accident.

Several months passed and the case was going cold. We wanted to stay but realized it was not possible. There was not enough work to be done to justify all the agents and troopers working on it full time. The plan was to send all of us back to

Harrisburg and leave only two FBI agents from the Philadelphia office and two state troopers assigned. A full-time prosecutor was assigned to the case in Harrisburg. His name was Rick Guida and oversaw the investigation. I knew Rick very well and we were friends, so I knew he would keep me informed.

Things were going very slowly and it was frustrating. During this time, I was transferred to Kentucky as Supervisor of the Covington office. Two years passed and finally enough evidence was collected to indict Bradfield for murder. Most of it was circumstantial but important enough to bring him to justice. Rick called me and told me that I was going to testify. I was subpoenaed for the state of Pennsylvania. It was going to be a difficult case, especially since the bodies of Karen and Michael had not been found. Bradfield did not testify on his own behalf. However, the jury found him guilty of the death of Susan Reinert and the deaths of Karen and Michael. He was later sentenced to three life terms in prison.

Four more years passed, and Smith had been indicted for murder and conspiracy to commit murder, and the state was seeking the death penalty. I had since been transferred to FBI Headquarters in Washington, D.C. I went to Harrisburg twice to meet with Rick Guida so he could brief me on the case, preparing me for my testimony.

Wendy Ziegler, Bradfield's lover who had accepted the $25,000 from Reinert, testified that Bradfield had told her that Smith was "mentally unstable," that he was intending to kill Susan, and that he had a list of others he wanted killed. Sue Meyers testified that Bradfield told her that "Dr. Smith intended to kill Susan Reinert." The truth of the matter was that Bradfield wanted Susan dead for her money and to avoid marrying her, and Smith owed him a favor after the alibi that Bradfield had provided in the Sears theft cases. We presumed Smith committed the murders on Bradfield's behalf.

After all the witnesses had testified for the prosecution and the defense, the jury deliberated on Smith's fate for two days. They found him guilty of the murders of Susan and her two children. The jury then had to decide the sentence, life or death. As they came back into the courtroom, the silence was deafening and eerie. Some of the jury members were crying. The foreman read the verdict to the judge and it was the death penalty. It was all over, or so I thought.

Before I say what happened next, I must mention the grandparents of Karen and Michael. They both attended every single day of Bradfield's and Smith's trials. They stayed at the same hotel we did. They often waited in the lobby to thank us for all our work. I thought of Karen and Michael knowing they would never see their grandparents again. It was heartbreaking.

I returned to FBI Headquarters in Washington. Bradfield was already serving his three life terms and Smith was on death row. About one year later I received a call from the Pennsylvania State Police Commissioner. I knew him and we talked for a few minutes. I wondered why he was calling, and I quickly realized it was not a social call. He began asking me about the case, specifically some of the evidence that had been collected. He also asked about Jack Holtz. I was really curious about what was going on. Jack had divorced his wife during the case. He had hired some state workers to move his belongings from his house. One of them was in the attic and dropped a box that fell open. Some papers fell to the floor and he went to pick them up. He noticed one that indicated Jack Holtz had been paid $50,000 by Joseph Wambaugh, who is a well-known true crime writer. The money was paid for information on the Reinert case during the course of testimony, and Wambaugh was able to author a book and a TV miniseries with the information from Holtz. The hired worker went to Smith's attorney, William Costopolus, and gave him the paperwork. Costopolus filed a suit for prosecutorial misconduct and asked the court for dismissal of all charges against Smith. The court also cited evidence suppression. Susan had sand on the soles of her feet, and it was known that Bradfield was at the beach the weekend of the murder. This supported the case for Smith's innocence.

The court ruled in Smith's favor, and after seven years on death row he was a free man. Jack Holtz left the State Police and later was sued by Smith. I was called to testify for the State, and I was furious with Holtz's conduct. It was terrible listening to him admit before the court everything he had done. I have never seen or spoken to him again.

In 1998, Bradfield was serving his three life terms in Graterford Prison. He had a heart attack, was sent to the hospital, and released after three days. He returned to prison and two of the state of Pennsylvania attorneys from Harrisburg went to see if he would tell what happen to Karen and Michael and where were they located. Bradfield simply shrugged his shoulders and would not say a word. One week later, he suffered a second heart attack and died.

Some years later, after I retired from the FBI, I decided to call Bill Costopolus. I knew him well. He was a former prosecutor who had gone into private practice, and was a good attorney. I asked Bill if it would be possible for me to talk to Smith. There was nothing I could do to change anything, but the thought of the fate of those two children had taken its toll on me. To this day, I think about them. Even if he did kill the children there was nothing I could do about it because double jeopardy applied and Smith couldn't be prosecuted even if he made a full confession. Bill chuckled and said he knew I was not going to do anything that was wrong. He said Smith did not talk to him, but he would ask. One week later, Bill emailed me and told me Smith said he would not talk to any FBI agent. I thanked Bill for trying and forgot about it.

Not long after that, I received a call from Costopolus and he said, "You are not going to believe this but Jay Smith said he would talk to you."

I was stunned. I flew to Harrisburg then took a rental car to Scranton, Pennsylvania where Smith was living at the time. I met him in a hotel restaurant. He said he did not know if he was going to talk to me or not and I said, "That's fine, I will leave." He changed his mind and sat down. I had already planned not to say anything about the case with the hopes I could build some rapport for a future visit. He began talking and I could not get many words in. I was working on my Ph.D., and he was fascinated by my research on leadership. We talked for four hours and I did not mention the case, but he did and denied having anything to do with Susan Reinert's death or the disappearance of her children. I quickly asked what he thought about the whereabouts of the children but said he did not know.

When we both got up to leave he said, "Do you want to get breakfast tomorrow?" I said,

"Yes." The next morning, we talked for a couple of hours and he asked If I was coming back. I told him I would. I arrived home and immediately began preparing questions, thinking there would be another visit. He called and sent cards to me which made me think I might have a possibility of finding out something about the children. In his last call he asked me when I was coming back. I said I would make flight reservations right away. He told me he had a doctor's appointment the next day but would be available afterwards. Before the day was over, I received a call from a former agent telling me Jay Smith was dead of a heart attack. I was the last FBI agent to talk to him. It haunts me that we will probably never know what happen to Michael and Karen.

CHAPTER 9:
THE CHARLIE SHOR
KIDNAPPING, 1982

It came time for me to be transferred again. I had the option to put my name on an Office of Preference request, meaning that if there was an opening in an office I wanted I could possibly be assigned there. I was contacted by Headquarters saying I was number one on the list to go to Louisville, Kentucky. I was reluctant to say yes as I really enjoyed the Harrisburg office. I decided I was going to take my name off the list and stay in Harrisburg. I called the Special Agent in Charge of the Louisville and advised him that I was going decline taking the transfer. He was not happy. He told me if I would come and work one of the high-profile cases pending in the office, I would have a good shot at being appointed Supervisor in Covington, Kentucky. That made me pause. Becoming supervisor was a big step up. After talking to Ann about it, I changed my mind back and took the transfer. She was excited to get home to Kentucky and her family.

I arrived in Louisville and was assigned a major case involving gambling and corruption. Six months passed and I was able to put together the case with the help of several agents in the office. I also worked with the local police in Louisville who had been trying to penetrate this criminal operation for some time. With the assistance of many officers we were able to plan and execute a raid on over thirty establishments that were running illegal gambling operations.

I was then asked if I would work a case as an undercover operative in Covington and Newport, Kentucky, both of which were just across the Ohio River from Cincinnati and were hotbeds of gambling, prostitution, and corruption. I was able to get close to several individuals who were conducting illegal businesses. I was introduced to a man named Buck who was well known as a veteran criminal. He lived in Newport and ran an adult bookstore. We hit it off and became friends, or so he thought.

Buck wanted me to set up a gambling operation in his home with me as the bookie, taking bets on just about everything. I knew nothing about being a bookie. The FBI in Quantico sent an expert on gambling to teach me how to do this. It was not easy. Buck set up a phone in his house on the second floor. I took bets, paid winners, and slept in one of his rooms. I was able to find out about all the other bookies and their addresses and numbers. We had enough evidence to shut down several establishments and arrest many bookies. About twenty-five agents conducted the raid, and almost a hundred suspects were arrested and charged.

I remained in the Covington office and soon was appointed Supervisor. My family and I lived in a house in Cincinnati, Ohio, just across the Ohio River and a few miles away. My first few months there were not as smooth as I would have liked. I had been in the bureau for ten years.

There were agents in the office that had over twenty-five years and some I believe resented me being their supervisor. I ignored most of the ones who complained and continued doing what I had been doing all along, which was work hard and set a good example. There was tension at times but for the most part we had a good office with competent agents.

I had been the supervisor of the Covington office for about five months when I received a call at 2:00 AM. At that time of the morning, I knew there was something going on that could not be good. The call was from an agent who was at the Covington police department. He said there was a possible kidnapping that had occurred but he was not sure it was legitimate. I told him I was on the way. When I arrived, Agent Pat Conley told me he had spoken to a gentleman who worked security for a major company in the Covington area, Duro Bag Manufacturing Company. The security officer told us the CEO, David Shor, had received a call demanding ransom for the safe return of his son, Charlie. Charlie's mother had first answered . When she heard the demand, she became very upset and gave the phone to her husband. The caller said they had his son and demanded $250,000 for his return. The caller said not to contact the FBI or any law enforcement or Charlie would die.

Charlie worked for the company as the President and Chief Operating Officer. His salary was very close to the amount being demanded, which was strange. It suggested that the kidnappers knew more about their subject than if they had just pulled his name out of the phone book.

This was not something that could be ignored, so I called all the Covington agents and asked them to report to the office as soon possible. By the time everyone arrived it was about 5:00 AM. We went to work contacting friends, co-workers, and family to see if they knew the whereabouts of Charlie Shor. We came up with nothing, and he could not be found. I called the Louisville office of the FBI, alerting them that we would need some help. I also called the Cincinnati office for assistance. David lived in Cincinnati and Charlie lived in Hebron, Kentucky. By this time, we knew this was no joke.

The kidnapper told David Shor he would call again at 9:00 PM. David was told to go to a phone booth in Bellevue, Kentucky for instructions on where to deliver the money. David told the caller that his son needed daily medication or he would become very ill.

We planned the rest of the day with the priority being Charlie's safe return. We contacted the phone company for help and obtained a court order for permission to trace calls. We sent up an FBI plane with agents to take pictures of the area so that we knew it as well as the kidnappers. These were not digital pictures but needed to be brought back to a photo lab and developed, which took time. When we had the photos in hand, we realized how close the phone booth was to the Ohio River. Thinking that may be an escape route, we asked the Coast Guard for assistance. This would turn out to be a good move. We told David we would put together the ransom with tracking devices and only a few bills that were real but mostly fake money. David would have none of that. He did not want to take a chance of anything going wrong that may endanger his son's life. After some negotiating, we agreed to follow his lead. David was also insistent that he drive his own vehicle to the drop point. We asked him to let us put an agent in as the driver and he refused that as well. We were able to at least convince him to put an agent on the floor in the backseat of his car. It would have to be enough.

It is important to note that the Shor family and Duro didn't exactly have $250,000 in cash in a vault somewhere. Not even close. David had to go to the bank and get a loan for the money. Fortunately for all of us, David had very good credit and they loaned him the cash without asking questions.

We had fifty agents available for surveillance. Those were the days of phone booths, so we prepared a map of the locations of the booths in two cities. We had two agents set up in a car on every phone booth. The one the kidnappers ordered David to go to was wired to enable us to hear both sides of the conversation. At that point, it was all we could do until we made contact with the kidnappers.

I made the difficult decision not to inform any other law enforcement agencies of the kidnapping. Our relationship with the local police was strong, but we could not take a chance of word getting out from them and endangering

Charlie or getting him killed. Police officers all had radios on their belts as well as in their cars, and many civilians had scanners set to those frequencies. They would be able to hear any traffic about Charlie's kidnapping. This would be very bad for Charlie. The FBI radio frequencies on the other hand are not known to the public for exactly that reason. This was a controversial decision, as we really needed as many agents and officers available as possible to make sure we caught the kidnappers. It weighed heavily on me. If I called it wrong, my decision to play this close to the chest could cost Charlie his life.

All units were in place at 8:00 PM, and I was near the designated phone booth in my vehicle. At 8:45, David, with $250,000 cash and an agent on the floor of his car, entered the phone booth. The phone rang at 9:00 PM sharp and David answered. The caller told him to go to another phone two blocks away for further instructions. We thought they may leapfrog like that to see if he was being followed and to frustrate any attempts to listen in. As the caller was talking to David, two agents who were stationed at a nearby booth saw an individual talking on the phone. The agents had seen this individual enter the booth at about five minutes before nine. At 9:00 PM the suspect was seen dialing the phone. We wondered how many times this was going to happen. During the call, David demanded he get his son back. The caller asked if he had the money and he said yes. The caller said, "When we get the money, you'll get your son back." He gave David the location of another phone booth and hung up.

David got into his car and drove to the second location. We had agents watching this booth and saw him enter. The suspect was seen walking to a different booth. He looked as though he was biding his time and was seen urinating in the booth. He also had something in his hand but the agents could not tell what it might be. The suspect made the call to David at the new location and told him to drive to Route 8 which ran along the shore of the Ohio River for many miles, then to stop and park near an overpass. By this time, it was getting dark, and surveillance was going to be very difficult. The suspect left the phone booth to proceed to the drop point, and immediately agents began processing it for fingerprints and other evidence. Sitting on the shelf was what looked like a walkie-talkie but turned out to be a scanner set to police frequencies. My call not to inform the police was correct.

It was a two-lane road and the agent on the floor was communicating via radio to us the best he could without being heard or seen. Several of us took up trying to follow David's car. Our headlights were making it very difficult for us to stay unseen. We heard David say he was stopping the car at the overpass. His car was wired so we could hear him or anyone else. The suspect had apparently run out of the woods from near the Ohio River to the Shor car. A voice was heard saying, "Where's the money?" David replied, "Where's my son?" He then began calling out Charlie's name. We decided to move in at that point, and our cars were approaching rapidly towards the scene. The suspect ran towards the river and jumped in the water, swimming downstream. The Coast Guard was alerted and sped to the location. They lit up the area where the suspect was swimming. He exited the water, ran up the bank, and was captured by waiting agents.

Meanwhile, Charlie had been tied to a nearby tree and was able to free himself. He ran toward his father, coming from the same direction the suspect had gone. He got into his father's car. With the FBI escorting them, they drove quickly to our office where our medics could evaluate Charlie without the chaos of a hospital.

The suspect was 23-year-old Christopher Meyers from Cincinnati, Ohio. He was processed, fingerprinted, photographed, and interviewed. He readily wanted to talk and did so without an attorney. He told us the other person involved was Bruce Pille, also 23, from Dayton, Kentucky. With the name of the second suspect identified, the Dayton Police was able to arrest him about four hours later as he was leaving his house. He too was brought to our office.

Charlie Shor was a muddy mess and very upset. He just wanted to go home. We all understood but needed to interview him while everything was still fresh in his mind. However, he was in no condition to talk so we decided to wait until the following day. He told me he did not want to prosecute anyone. I told him that would not be possible as they had committed a serious crime. Agents escorted both Charlie and his father to David's home.

The two suspects were interviewed and both cooperated. We learned they had planned this for a long time. Bruce Pille was an employee at Duro and was the ringleader. Christopher Meyer was the son of a Cincinnati fireman, and neither one had a criminal record. Individually, they told the story of the kidnapping. The two planned to kidnap Charlie Shor and demand a ransom of $250,000 from Charlie's father. They went to great lengths to make their plan work. They spent several days at A.J. Jolly State Park digging a deep pit to secure the victim. This was a curious choice of location since the park isn't very big and there is usually a lot of activity. They also took great pains to build a camouflage cover for the pit.

Charlie lived alone on a farm in northern Kentucky. The driveway to the house was very long and wooded, and the farmhouse was not visible to any road. Pille and Meyer went to Charlie's home when he was away and scoped out their plan. They even did dry runs. They picked the day based on Pille's knowledge of Charlie's schedule.

The night of the kidnapping came and the two hid in the woods. They put a bicycle in the driveway so that Charlie would have to get out of his car to move it. When Charlie got out of the car, one of the two men put a gun up to Charlie's head, and the other brandished a knife. They told him if he did anything to resist, he would be killed. They grabbed Charlie, handcuffed him, and put him in the backseat of his own car. They constantly threatened to kill him. Charlie shouted, "If you kill me, you're going to get the death penalty." One of them laughed, "No one gets the death penalty." Pille and Meyer had a motorcycle hidden in the woods for their transportation. One drove Charlie's car and the other drove the motorcycle to a waiting car. They put Charlie in the other car and abandoned his. They drove to the park where the hole had been dug. Charlie did not know where he was going as he was blindfolded.

They stopped, removed Charlie from the car, and walked him to the pit. They lowered him into it, blindfolded and gagged. They covered the hole with the camouflage and left the area. All of this occurred between 10:00 PM and midnight.

Charlie was given no food, no water, and no way to relieve himself. They knew Charlie had epilepsy. He was prone to seizures and without medicine he could die. This was not a problem for them. Charlie was buried alive, and his hands were fastened to a stake so he couldn't move. He was blindfolded and gagged. He sat in the pit all night and at daylight could hear someone walking around above him, most likely Meyers. Meanwhile, Pille went to work at Duro that morning to see if there was any word of Charlie's abduction. Not hearing anything, they proceeded with their ransom plan.

At about 8:00 PM the day after the abduction, they took Charlie from the pit to the drop site, near the river and Route 8, where they tied him to a tree and his handcuffs were removed. This is where the ransom drop was to happen. They had been waiting for hours before David showed up. When he heard his father's voice, Charlie was suddenly able to untie himself and run—Charlie attributes this to God—despite the kidnapper with the gun walking around him constantly. He tells me that "it was better to be shot than go through any more of the hell they put me through." Charlie had been subjected to almost a full day of torture, including being bitten by hundreds of bugs while he was in that pit. He was lucky he did not have a seizure. He was lucky to be alive. It was not surprising that he just wanted to go home.

After the interviews of Pille and Meyers were concluded, I went Pille's interview room and asked, "You want to tell me why you did this?" Pille looked up at me and said, "I needed the money so I could go to bible college in Oklahoma." I replied, "You have got to be kidding me." I said to myself that he would have plenty of time to read the bible in prison.

Both Pille and Meyers pled guilty to kidnapping and other charges. The judge gave them the maximum sentence he could give, twenty years with no possibility of parole.

Charlie and I have been friends for some time. He had difficulty living with this ordeal. It was remarkable he survived without his medication. Charlie was able to become a tremendous businessman, building the largest bag company in the world, employing over 2,500 people. We see and talk to one another frequently and I am grateful for his friendship.

CHAPTER 10:
THE WEBER PHARMACY
MURDER, 1986

One Sunday morning in December 1986, I was reading the newspaper when I noticed an article about a robbery/homicide in a small town in Kentucky. It involved narcotics, which brought it under federal jurisdiction. As I read further, I learned the robbery had taken place in a small pharmacy in Bellevue, Kentucky, just on the other side of the Ohio River from Cincinnati. The owner of the pharmacy had been killed. The Chief of Police in Dayton, Kentucky, which had jurisdiction, was Elmer Corbin, a man I knew well. The FBI office was closed on weekends, and I was not the duty agent on call so I wasn't responsible for following up on the case. I figured one of the other agents was handling it.

The following Monday I arrived at the office about 7:30 AM. The supervisor was standing in the doorway to his office, and I asked who was investigating the Weber Pharmacy. He said no one. I asked him why, but he simply shrugged. "Do you want the case?" he asked. Of course I did. Although I didn't say anything, I wondered to myself if my supervisor knew about the federal narcotics violation. It didn't matter at that point, of course. I was on the case and I knew about it.

As I drove the few miles to the Dayton Police Department, I thought about how to approach the chief. I did not want to take the case away from him. I had learned this lesson after many years of working with local law enforcement agencies, particularly in Harrisburg. My approach was to offer assistance, but only if they wanted it.

I walked into the department and found the Chief of Police sitting at his desk. This department had six officers and only one was a detective. I asked him about the case and who was working the investigation. Like my own supervisor, he merely shrugged. I asked him, "Do you need some help?" He replied, "I sure do." He gave me an office to use, and he and the detective briefed me on what had happened at the pharmacy.

At about 10:30 Saturday morning, two male individuals ran into Weber Pharmacy and announced, "Give us all the schedule one narcotics." Both were disguised with hats, gloves, and sunglasses. Mr. Weber and his employee, a young man named David, were alone there. One of the individuals covered Mr. Weber and David with a handgun and the other ordered David to the floor. He began taping David's hands and feet. They had taken their attention off of Mr. Weber, an oversight that would cost one of the robbers and Mr. Weber their lives.

Mr. Weber was standing in front of a cabinet, watching David being taped up. The individual with the gun began ransacking the cabinets for narcotics. While both men were distracted, Mr. Weber, who had his hands behind his back, was able to retrieve a pistol from a drawer in the cabinet behind him. About six months prior, Mr. Weber had brought a small pistol after the pharmacy had been robbed of narcotics. Mr. Weber pointed his gun in the direction of the male taping his employee and said, "You are not taking a damn thing out of here." With that the suspect lunged at Weber and hit him in the face. As they struggled, Mr. Weber fired his pistol at the individual, hitting him in the chest. The bullet severed his aorta, causing severe bleeding, and the injured robber started falling to the floor. The coroner said he lived for only about sixty seconds with that type of wound. Meanwhile, the suspect with the gun immediately fired his gun and hit Mr. Weber in his side. Mr. Weber was gravely wounded. This all happened so quickly that when Mr. Weber fell to the floor, the wounded suspect fell on top of him. The other suspect ran from the store to a waiting car and driver and sped away from the scene.

The employee was able to get out of his bonds and call 9-1-1. He also called Mrs. Weber, who ran towards the store. The Webers lived only two blocks away. Shortly thereafter, a police officer ran into the store. Mrs. Weber was already there, kneeling and holding the hands of her husband, crying loudly. David pulled the now-dead suspect away from Mr. Weber who was having trouble breathing. Mr. Weber could be heard saying, "God have mercy on my soul." He knew he was dying. Mrs. Weber cried, "Why didn't you give them what they wanted?" Observing the scene, the officer saw that Mr. Weber was in great distress and ran to his car to radio the ambulance that had been dispatched. "Expedite, expedite," he called, and returned to assist Mr. Weber.

The ambulance arrived quickly, tending to Mr. Weber the best they could. He was put into the ambulance and they sped off to the hospital. According to the ambulance attendant, Mr. Weber managed to whisper once again, "God have mercy on me." He died before they arrived at the hospital.

The small pharmacy had been torn apart during the robbery. The floor was covered with blood, prescription bottles both filled and empty, scraps of paper, and overturned cabinets. The detective said they put all the items into bags as evidence. The blood was cleaned off the floor with a firehose.

The chief said they were able to identify the subject that was shot and killed but had not been able to identify Mr. Weber's killer or the driver of the getaway vehicle. The deceased robber was Charles Lake, a resident of Dayton, Kentucky. He had a criminal record and just six months prior had been released from prison after serving a sentence for robbery and theft. Chief Corbin ask me to take over the case and his department would assist. I knew there were going to be a lot of interviews, so I asked for help from the FBI office. One agent came to assist me. The police had been to the home where Lake lived and found he was staying with a woman and her sister and several children. The interview was not productive according to the detective, who said he thought Charles Lake's girlfriend was not being truthful and did not want to be involved. I went to the home with the detective and got a similar response.

I returned to the police department and began inspecting the evidence taken from the pharmacy. We went through the bags. Everything was covered in dried blood. The smell was unbearable. It was very sad to see all this, and it turned out there was nothing that could help us.

The Monday after the robbery, a Dayton police officer interviewed a citizen who had allegedly saw the suspect run out of the pharmacy and get into an orange-colored car. He had noted the license number and gave it to the officer. The plate read J8M-BIH and the witness said it was an Ohio tag, white with green letters. I ran the tag number and it was registered to a car with an address of a residence six hours away from Dayton, Kentucky. We were reasonably certain that was not the car, but it was the only lead we had. We went back to the man that saw the car and he was positive he wrote down the number correctly. I asked for an agent to locate the vehicle and interview the owner. He got back to me right away and said this could not be the suspect as the car had not been driven for some time and the owner was an elderly man who rarely went anywhere.

I returned to the Lake residence with the detective. We were determined to get to the truth. We politely told them that withholding evidence is a federal crime with serious repercussions. Lake's girlfriend began crying, saying she did not want to get involved. We explained to her she was already involved but by telling us the truth she may not be charged with a crime.

We learned a lot during that interview. For example, we discovered that Charles Lake had a sister, Shay Lake, who was living in Kentucky. Her boyfriend, a man named Harry Smith, was from Ohio. We learned Smith had come to Charles Lake's house the morning of the robbery. We found out Smith drove a small orange car. We also learned that a man named Jackie Warren had come to the house that morning and the three of them had been in the garage for several hours. With this information, we returned to the police department to sort everything out. I was not convinced she had yet told us everything but we had enough to go on for the moment. Besides, we could always go back if we needed more information.

There was talk between the prosecutors, federal and state, of seeking the death penalty for the murder of Mr. Weber. The federal government did not have the death penalty in force at that time, but the state of Kentucky did have that option. It was agreed that the federal government would prosecute the narcotics robbery and then the state would try the death penalty case.

We worked on this day and night. Around 8:00 PM one evening, a police officer came to us and said there was a lady and an eleven-year-old boy who wanted to talk to the FBI. I was just about to go home, but the officer said she was insisting that they talk to us. The boy was clearly scared. The mother said he had something to say involving the Weber case. I crouched down next to him and asked softly if he would tell me what he knew. He said he and a friend were playing on the bank of the Ohio river. He said it was Saturday, the day of the robbery. He noticed a car driving very fast towards them. He and his friend got behind a tree to hide. The car was orange and one man got out of the car, ran to the shoreline, and threw a gun in the river. The boy said that before throwing the gun, the man opened the cylinder and took out the bullets. He saw the man throw the gun, bullets, and cylinder into the water.

It was quite late, well after dark, but I asked him if he could show us where all of this had occurred. He said he would. We drove to the river and he pointed to the spot where the man threw the gun in the river. A decision was made to use police divers to see if they could retrieve the gun. It was about midnight when they arrived. Three divers donned their suits ready to enter cold, dirty, water that was twenty feet over its normal level. Each diver had a lifeline for safety and could communicate to police personnel from under the water. The divers could not see, so they had to use their hands to feel the bottom of the riverbed. Things were going well enough until an alert was heard from one of the divers. He was caught underneath a tree and could not free himself. I was in a panic. The handlers were able to retrieve him, and I called the search off for fear of losing one of the divers.

Although I needed the gun, I had to put this on hold for a while. I located Jackie Warren, and not surprisingly, he was less than cooperative. I told him I thought he was involved and I planned to prove it; it was his choice whether to cooperate or not. He was not under arrest at that time, so there was nothing I could do to compel him to work with us.

I also located Shay Lake, Charles' sister. She refused to say anything—at least, anything helpful. She did a lot of talking, but most of it was cursing us out. She had the foulest mouth I have ever heard. I then returned to Charles Lake's girlfriend and told her this was the last chance to come clean. I asked if there were any drugs in the house and she went to the basement and brought up a bag full of marijuana. This was good, she was cooperating. She told me that, on the day of the robbery, Harry Smith had come to their house and drove his orange car into their garage. Surprised, I asked what happened to the car and she said it was still there. I didn't have a search warrant for her home. I asked for written permission to search the garage and the house. She agreed and signed the release. I entered the garage and the orange car was there. I looked over the vehicle and noticed the license plate. Something was odd about it. I took the plate and had the car towed to a police lot for evidence. At the office, I looked closely at the plate and it read J3M-BTH. There was something wrong as there was a green substance on the plate, and it seemed as though it had been wiped clean. I decided to send it to the FBI laboratory for examination. The technician telephoned me and said he could see some type of green substance under the microscope but could not identify what it was. He said if I could find a likely candidate, he would be able to compare it to whatever was on the plate.

I returned to Lake's girlfriend's house again and asked if there was anything in the house that was green, though I really didn't know what I was asking for. I did not have to go further, however, because as soon as I said green she got up from the kitchen table and went to a cabinet. She opened the door and handed me a box of PAAS coloring, the type used for Easter eggs. I opened the box and there were several colors. I found the one that was green. It was the only one that had been opened. Before I left, Lake's girlfriend said she knew Jackie Warren was involved but did not know what he did. I took the box to the office and marked it as evidence. I called the technician and told him I was sending a tube of green coloring to him for examination. The evidence went to the lab via overnight mail.

Two days later I received a call from the lab technician. He said, "That's it, it was the substance on the license plate, and it had been wiped off." He also informed me that the car belonged to Harry Smith's mother, Shirley. Things were coming together for us. It had been two weeks of non-stop investigation, and now I believed we had it. I was bound and determined that we were going to get the robbers that murdered Mr. Weber.

I went to see Shay Lake and told her we needed to talk, that I had evidence that she knew something about the robbery she was not telling. An agent accompanied me to help with the interview. I asked Lake if she would be willing to come with us to the police department and she agreed. This was very late in the evening and she was denying any knowledge of the robbery. She did say that she and Harry Smith were close friends but that was it. She ranted with foul language, complaining about the police, the FBI, and whatever else she could think of. She said her brother was dead for no reason. I advised her she was not under arrest and she could leave anytime she wanted. She continued to talk, and this went on for several hours while we sat and listened. At about 4:00 AM, she began crying and said she would tell us what she knew.

Harry Smith had telephoned her the day of the robbery asking her to come to get him at Charles Lake's house. She drove him to Cincinnati where he lived with his mother. Along the way, Smith told her what had happened. Shay said

Smith made a statement, "I avenged Chuck," her brother. He said he shot the old man after her brother had been shot and killed. She dropped Smith off at his house and had not seen him since then. Shay said she would testify at a trial if necessary.

I knew there were blank spots in my case. I needed to talk to Jackie Warren, and I needed to get the gun that had been thrown in the river. After the first attempt to find the gun, everyone said it would be impossible to recover it.

I went to see Warren and asked him if he would come to the police department for an interview. He agreed. I told him I knew he was involved in the robbery and informed him of his right to remain silent. I laid out what I knew. I told him I knew he was the driver of the getaway car. I knew he was not involved in the murder, but I needed to know from him why was he driving the car. He refused to say anything and said he wanted an attorney. He still wasn't under arrest, so he left. As he was leaving, I told him this was the last time I would speak to him. I decided to ask the U.S. Attorney for an arrest warrant for Warren, as I knew I had enough probable cause.

The U.S. Attorney came through and I asked two agents from the office to make the arrest, thinking that Warren may talk to someone other than me.

The very next morning, after Warren had been arrested, I received a phone call from an attorney who said he was representing Jackie Warren. He asked if I would be willing to talk to him and if there would be any consideration given, even though he knew it would have to come from the court and not me. I said Warren must tell the truth and be willing to testify, if necessary, and they agreed. I met the attorney at the Kenton County Jail where Warren was housed. Warren was brought to the room, sat down, and I asked him to read and sign the waiver of rights. He did so and his attorney signed as well.

I let Warren talk while I took notes about the robbery and how he got involved. He told me he had received a phone call from Charles Lake on Saturday morning, the day of the robbery. Lake told Warren to come to his girlfriend's garage. Warren arrived and saw Harry Smith doing something with the license plate on an orange car. Warren ask what was going on. Lake told Warren that since Warren owed Lake some money from a recent marijuana sale, Lake would eliminate the debt for driving the car to the Weber pharmacy. Warren said this was crazy as the pharmacy was too close to where they lived. Lake ordered him to drive the car. Warren watched as Lake and Smith disguised themselves with grease in their hair, sunglasses, gloves, and hats. He drove them to the pharmacy and was told to pull into the alley beside the store and keep the car running. The two of them went into the store and both had guns. It was not very long before Smith ran out, jumped into the car, and said "Drive!" Warren asked, "What happen to Chuck?" Smith said "The old man shot him, and I shot the old man."

Smith told Warren to drive to the river. When they got there, Smith jumped out of the car, ran to the bank, and threw the gun, cylinder, and bullets into the water. Warren then drove to Lake's house and parked the car in the garage. Warren left and walked home but did not know what Smith was going to do.

I still needed to try to retrieve the pistol used in the robbery. I knew, however, it may not be possible. I had the bullet that had killed Mr.

Weber and wanted to find the gun for a match. Everyone thought I was crazy to even attempt to find a small gun in a large river, especially since the first effort had failed. One of the agents in the office suggested I call the Coast Guard to see if they could help. I did and was told there was a salvage operator, Captain James Beatty, about an hour down river who may be able to do something. I drove to his home and told him my problem. He said he had an electromagnet he used for getting large items from the river, boats and cars primarily. He said he would try for us.

It was the day after Christmas that Captain Beatty was to arrive. It took him all day to get up the river due to the heavy current. I met him at the designated spot. We were not able to try that day as it was too dark, so we met again the next morning. I showed him the area we thought the gun was located and he began setting up. It took one hour for him to get in position. It was very cold, and I was freezing but anxious. I started a fire on the bank to try to keep warm. Captain Beatty climbed up the ladder to the cab on the crane and lowered the magnet in the water. Whatever he brought up was dropped on a barge and two employees would filter the contents, looking for the gun.

He searched for four hours, then stopped and had lunch on his boat. It dawned on me then that the spot I had told him to search was too far out, a hundred feet away from the riverbank. I asked him if he could move the operation closer to the shore. He was not happy but agreed. This took another hour. He climbed up the ladder and swung the magnet around facing the shore and dropped it. He pulled it out of the water and released the contents onto the barge. The two employees started waving to me. I ran onto the barge, and there it was, just as the young boy described it. There was no cylinder in the gun, but that was fine as the lab only needed the barrel for comparison, not the cylinder. They would be able to use another cylinder to fire and examine the barrel and slug. I was very happy. I packaged the gun and rushed it to the lab. The technician was able to confirm the bullet from Weber came from the gun we retrieved. What a relief.

We now had to find and arrest Harry Smith. I obtained a warrant and the Cincinnati agents located his mother's house, confirmed he was inside and cleared the neighborhood. They ordered Smith to come out. He did not surrender so the swat team entered and began searching. One agent looked in a closet and found Smith on the top shelf, pulled him down, and placed him under arrest. Smith was not allowed bond, which meant he stayed in jail until the trial. He pled not guilty.

Several months passed before the trial was to begin. Prior to that, the prosecutor requested a model of the inside of the pharmacy to be built for the judge and jury to see. A team of specialists from the FBI came to Covington to get photos and measurements to build a mockup. It was a great prop for the trial as the jury members were able to see what happened that day. Smith was found guilty in the federal case and sentenced to life plus 35 years, and found guilty by the state but sentenced to life and not the death penalty.

CHAPTER 11:
THE KENTUCKY BANK GANG,
1989

In the late 1980s, the Covington area was getting hit with bank robberies way out of proportion with the national average. We could not get a good handle on solving these robberies due to a lack of evidence. We knew how they were pulling them off, but we couldn't get any leads on who it was that was committing them. This is how it usually came down: A gang of five robbers would steal a vehicle. Then, on a Friday—always a Friday—four of them would enter the bank wearing masks and gloves, three with bags to carry the money out and one who stood at the door with a stopwatch. One robber would target the vault while the two others would clean out the tellers. At exactly two minutes they would exit the bank to the waiting vehicle with the fifth member of the gang driving. Within a few miles or minutes of the bank, they would abandon the stolen vehicle and get into another car that had been placed in a safe area. We knew their MO backwards and forwards, but it did us absolutely no good. Five banks had been robbed like this in the northern Kentucky area and we could not identify any of the suspects. These thieves were slick, very professional, and I was getting frustrated. I worked day and night to come up with anything that would help me get these guys. Every interview I conducted was negative as far as leads or evidence goes.

Every time there was a bank robbery nearby, our field offices would be notified, giving detailed information about the robbery, whether it had been solved or not. On a hunch, I began reading about robberies in the general area and noticed that there were several cases in surrounding states that were like the ones in Kentucky. I telephoned an agent in Ohio to ask about details of their robbery. They had two unsolved cases that closely matched ours. The agent told me he knew other states were having the same problem, specifically Indiana and Tennessee. I contacted each of the offices in those states to compare similarities between the cases. We decided to get together to discuss the robberies and share any information that would help all of us.

We began to see that the robberies always followed the same MO. It was clear that we were seeing one gang, not several copycats. By the time we met, this gang had obtained over $2 million. None of the other agents I met with had any more information than I did. We knew how they did it, but not who. We were eager to get these guys. Something had to break.

I had an informant, a lady I had arrested for bad checks, who was well known in the criminal community and knew just about all of the thieves and lowlifes in the city of Covington. I was paying her for information she provided, as long as it resulted in an arrest, was legitimate, and was accurate. I had been very nice to her as she was my eyes and ears on crime in the city.

I asked her if she knew anything about the bank robberies that had occurred in the area. She didn't, but did mention a names of a couple of former bank robbers. Billy Gaston was a known criminal and had a long list of crimes he had committed. He had been in and out of prison too many times to count. My informant told me he was originally from Cuba and was a "bad dude." At one point he had been arrested for assaulting a former girlfriend. During sex, she had angered him, so he bit off her nipple. From what she told me, he was a complete sociopath.

The other former bank robber was Elmer Edwards. Although she had not seen Edwards for some time, she said he was "trouble" and into just about anything. The informant also told me she would frequently see Gaston and Edwards together in a bar in the city. There was another individual often seen with them, a tall guy, but she did not know his name. I asked her to see if she could find out the name and let me know.

I finally had leads on some possible suspects. I researched their criminal background, confirming the information she had provided. That was a start and as it turned out, a huge help.

My informant was one of the most fearless individuals in the city. The next time the tall guy came into the bar, she went up to him and asked him to buy her a drink. After a couple of beers, she was able to get his name, Jesse Adams. I ran his name and found out he had a criminal record as long as my arm, another bad dude. I had not heard about Adams prior to this but was talking with another agent in the Covington office and mentioned his name. The agent had heard of him and told me Adams had previously been identified in a case belonging to the agent, and said this was a "nasty guy." Hearing all of this, I knew I was not dealing with choir boys.

Later, on a Friday, a call came into our office that a robbery had occurred in a suburb of Covington. We rushed to the scene but of course the robbers and money were gone. As soon as we began interviewing the bank personnel, it became obvious it was our gang of robbers raising their ugly heads again. It same MO and no evidence, and no way to identify the robbers. The bank was located near a shopping mall and local police were helping with the investigation.

We were just about finished processing the scene when a police officer came to me and handed me a napkin that had a license plate number written on it. The officer said he was driving though the mall parking lot, and an elderly man got out of a car and waved him down. The individual told the officer he was sitting in his car, waiting for his wife to return, when another vehicle pulled into a vacant parking space directly in front. The gentleman saw four individuals quickly get out of the car, removing masks and carrying bags, and get into a vehicle next to the one they had exited. The witness said he slid down in the seat for fear of being noticed. As the four individuals backed out, he grabbed a napkin and wrote down the license plate number. Finally, a break in the case.

I returned to the office and ran the plate. It was registered to a Cathy Jones. I had no idea who this was, but we had and address and description of the car that matched what the elderly man had told the officer.

We decided to set up surveillance on the address to see who was going in and out. Early one morning, two agents from the office accompanied me there. It turned out to be a condominium. We set up in different locations to observe. One agent immediately identified the vehicle associated with the license plate. We sat for about an hour with no movement. Then one of the agents noticed a delivery truck drive into the area and stop in front the address we were watching. We observed two men get out of the truck, open the back, and carry a large television into Cathy Jones' residence. The delivery men exited and drove away. I radioed one of the surveillance cars and asked for him to follow them some distance away from the condo and stop the delivery truck to ask who and what had occurred. After speaking with them, the agents asked them both to come to the police department.

We learned that a large screen TV had been purchased and a man in the condominium paid cash on delivery for the set. The money had red dye on some of the bills and smelled of what we knew to be tear gas. We also identified several bills that matched the bait money stolen during the robbery three days before. We now knew there were two people in the condo, Cathy Jones and an unidentified male. With the evidence we had I asked the U.S. Attorney for a search warrant for the residence. A federal judge authorized the warrant.

We decided we would execute the warrant the following day at 6:00 AM. The local police accompanied us to the residence, and we got into place. I went to the front door with the Chief of Police. We knocked loudly and announced ourselves as law enforcement officers. No response. We tried again and no response. Last try, we announced ourselves and said we were going to kick the door in. No one came to the door. Two police officers brought up the battering ram and began pounding the door. It was about halfway open when from upstairs a female hollered down to us that she would open the door. It was a little late at that point. There wasn't much of the door left since we had hit it hard.

The female and she said she was Cathy Jones. We asked for identification, and I asked if there was anyone else home and she said there was, upstairs. One of the agents went upstairs and found a male individual and brought him to the main floor. We separated them both and interviewed them while police officers and agents searched through the condo. We learned the male was named Rodney Starkey. He as unknown to us. Shortly, a police officer brought down a jacket from upstairs. We went through the pockets and found numerous bills that smelled of tear gas and were covered with red dye.

Starkey was advised of his rights and he refused to cooperate. One of the agents continued to talk with him and Starkey agreed to maybe cooperate if he would get some leniency. I called the U.S. Attorney and told him of what we found, and that Starkey said he would talk. The attorney said he would consider this, but the judge had the final say. We arranged for Starkey to come to the federal building to talk with the Assistant U.S. Attorney. I knew we could have asked for a warrant and arrested him right away but I also knew we still had four or five other individuals out there somewhere set to continue robbing banks.

Starkey came to see us and we asked him to talk about the robberies and the names of the individuals involved. He was told that for any consideration he must tell about every robbery he participated in, and he would be required to testify for the government. We told him he also must let us know if there were plans for future robberies. Then and only then would he be given leniency. Nevertheless, the judge would be the final voice.

Starkey agreed and told us he was involved in three bank robberies. He also named the other individuals: Jesse Adams, Billy Gaston, and Elmer Edwards were involved in all of them. There were other fill ins, whose names he did not know. Starkey said the robberies were well d. He said Adams and Gaston were the ringleaders and they were based out of Covington. Starkey said there was a person who would steal vehicles for the robberies when asked by Gaston or Adams, and the cars were always Toyotas. Starkey would meet with the gang for coffee where plans were made for future robberies. Starkey knew something big was in the works soon but did not know for sure what it was. He said he would probably find out at the next meeting. We needed to know the cars they were currently using, and he identified them for us. We released him with the understanding that we had him, and if he wanted to keep the leniency deal he would have to continue to cooperate.

At the next meeting Starkey attended he learned of a robbery that was out of character.

They were planning to rob an armored car and were going to shoot the guard if necessary. This was the big time. Not just the vaults at a bank. They had already cased the area and planned this for an unknown date. Starkey said they were going to do a dry run the following Friday. He explained that each week an armored car would stop and take cash to two banks. One was on the side of the street the armored car parked, and the other bank was on the opposite corner. On the pushcarts was one million dollars, all wrapped up and ready to be taken.

I decided to film them casing the bank. We requested technicians from our office in Louisville to come to Covington with camera equipment for filming. There was a church across the street from the bank. From the church steeple we would able to film the entire intersection. I asked the Cincinnati office to send up a plane up for surveillance using our FBI pilot. We had several cars on the street watching the area. At about 9:00 AM, one of the agents radioed that he saw one of our suspect cars drive through the intersection with Billy Gaston in the front passenger seat. The FBI plane was notified and asked to take up surveillance on the car. The pilot was able to stay with the car, which allowed us to follow the Gaston vehicle at a good distance. The suspects were followed from Kentucky to a trailer on a piece of property in Rising Sun, Indiana, about 40 miles away by road from Covington. We found out later the location was where Elmer Edwards was staying.

Once we found this, we backed off and returned to our office. We all were on edge from that time forward as we did not know when the next robbery was going to happen, and we weren't entirely certain where either. The next Friday approached and I had learned nothing new from Starkey. I went to Covington, their meeting place, and drove around looking for any of their cars. As luck would have it, I found one. I sat on the car, a Volvo, and requested assistance. Soon someone got into the suspect vehicle and began driving. Another agent caught up with me and we tried to follow them. It was difficult as traffic was horrible, and these guys were trail conscious. They would exit one offramp and cross over to the onramp to see it they were being followed. Finally, with only two cars we were unable to keep up with them.

The following Monday, at about 9:00 AM, I received a call from an agent from Knoxville, Tennessee, 250 miles away. He had attended the meeting we had with agents from several states. He asked for the description of the car we had identified. I said it was a gray Volvo. He quickly responded, "The car is here and we are in a shootout right now. We have three suspects holed up in a house, one police officer has been shot and one FBI agent wounded." The suspects had robbed a bank and an off-duty police officer had seen them leave and followed them to the residence where they were now hiding. After a couple of hours, two suspects were allowed to come out of the house. They were a young male and female. The other individual in the house continued shooting. Finally, the man came out of the house, crawling on his back with a gun pointed at his own chest, threatening to commit suicide. An FBI sharpshooter went to the corner of the house with a rifle and shot the gun from the suspect's hand. He was immediately subdued and cuffed. It was none other than Jesse Adams. The police officer survived his wound and the agent was mostly unharmed. All of this was broadcast on local news and it was quite a headline and video.

The story was not over though, as there were several other robbers still at large—namely Billy Gaston and Elmer Edwards—somewhere in Kentucky or Indiana. Friday was approaching again with no guarantee whether they were going to hit, though now we had a pretty good idea of where. We were sure the next robbery was going to be the armored car. Every agent in the office was setting up surveillance in both Newport and Covington.

I was in Newport, Kentucky near the bar where they normally met. I had just bought a cup of coffee and a doughnut and was settling in for the surveillance. A couple of agents were near the banks where the armored car drivers made their "walk the money across the street" delivery. We were all in place by 7:00 AM. We thought we were early since the armored car didn't make its delivery until around 9:00 AM. I expected to be the first to have eyes on this crew. But it wasn't five minutes after my first sip of coffee that one of our first office agents, Connie Reid, radioed me asking for the license number of one of the suspect vehicles. I rattled it off and she replied, "I am right behind it at a traffic light." I threw my coffee and doughnut out and took off to the location. She said the car was travelling in the direction of the armored car corner. Once in the area I also saw the car. After the shootout the previous week in Tennessee, I was sure they were going to actually rob the armored car that day. I knew we could not let them go any farther. There was a genuine risk to the public and at any moment they could make our surveillance.

I radioed the secretary in our office to call the U.S. Attorney. Contrary to popular belief, we didn't have police radios in our cars, and they didn't have FBI frequencies on their radios. Using the office phone and our radio we relayed what was happening and asked for approval to make an immediate arrest, all while keeping them under surveillance. Even if we did not catch them in the process of a crime, we could possibly charge them with conspiracy to rob. We got our approval.

Our next dilemma was how to stop them. All our cars were unmarked. Trying to make a traffic stop in an unmarked car could present a real danger. There was no way to guarantee that the robbers would stop, and even if they did, the local civilians may not understand what was going on and possibly approach, thinking that the robbers needed help from the armed agents. If we had lights and sirens, everyone would know who was who, making the situation much less critical. I did not want a shootout in the middle of a very busy intersection.

I radioed the office secretary to request she contact the Covington Police Department. We communicated via FBI radio and the office phone to the dispatcher that we needed marked police units to assist us with a traffic stop. We relayed the information about the targets and shared their location as we continued to stay as far back as possible and trade positions to ensure we were not made.

I had an eye on the robbers as they circled the bank twice by going through an alley. A marked unit came up behind me. I motioned for him to stop the vehicle just ahead of me. He did and I jumped out of my car and yelled "FBI." I approached the passenger side with my gun drawn, and other agents surrounded the car. A man named Wayne McGinnis was driving, and

Billy Gaston was in the passenger seat. The police officer got McGinnis out of the car and I pulled Gaston out. Other agents were there and quickly cuffed them. I reached underneath the passenger seat and pulled out a loaded .45 caliber pistol with a round in the chamber. I guess my fears about the shootout were correct.

In the backseat was Elmer Edwards, who followed instructions to get out of the car with his hands up. All three were taken to the Covington Police Department for processing and interviews. As I was interviewing Gaston, which was going nowhere, the officer who'd transported Gaston knocked on the door. When I came out, he handed me what looked like a card key. He explained that before he begins a shift and after every transport of anyone in his car, he is required to inspect his vehicle for contraband. That included pulling out the backseat. There was nothing under the seat at the beginning of his shift. The first person who had been in the backseat of his car that morning had been Gaston. After pulling out Gaston and transferring him to lockdown, the officer once again searched his car and removed the backseat. He found the card key stuffed behind it. Although handcuffed from behind, Gaston had been able to remove the card key from his back pocket and hide it under the seat.

Of course, when asked, Gaston denied any knowledge of the key and refused to talk further. McGinnis and Edwards weren't talking either. The card key was identified as belonging to a storage unit. We contacted the owner of the company, who agreed to share his list of unit renters. We looked at the registration for names. Of all the luck, Billy Gaston had signed his own name.

We got a search warrant and went to the unit. There we hit pay dirt. We found masks, guns, stolen property, and money. It was all there. We then got a search warrant for the trailer in Indiana that we had identified during the aerial surveillance. Another success. It was full of evidence, masks, and newspaper articles from Knoxville, Tennessee with a picture of Jesse Adams.

We finally had Gaston as well as Elmer Edwards and McGinnis. We also got warrants and arrested Jerry Kidwell, the thief who had stolen the cars, and Elmer's grandson who drove the getaway car in some of the robberies, all with the help of local police and many FBI agents.

Billy Gaston pled guilty and was sentenced to 20 years. McGinnis pled guilty and was sentenced to 10 years. Kidwell provided substantial cooperation and received probation. Elmer's grandson pled guilty and got a minimal sentence. Elmer Edwards, who was 60 years old at the time, figured he had nothing to lose and went to trial. He was found guilty and sentenced to 25 years. Rodney Starkey testified for the government and was not charged with anything from the bank robberies. This was the biggest break I had ever seen anyone get and he walked out a free man.

This, however, was not the end of the story. Six months later, as I was sitting at my desk a call came in about a bank robbery in a small town, Cold Spring, Kentucky, on the outskirts of Covington. A first office agent responded along with local police. The agent returned to the office and told me the story. It had been a one-man robbery. The robber was disguised and got very little money. This small town had only two officers, and right before the robbery they received a call to respond to a fight that was occurring at the bowling alley at the one end of the town. The officers had no idea the bank was being robbed.

While the agent was telling what had happened I asked if he had retrieved the tape recording of the call to the dispatcher about the fight. It was standard procedure to tape all calls that came into the police. He said no and I asked him to go get it. He did and upon her return, we played the tape. After hearing three words, I said, "That is Rodney Starkey." I told the agent to ask for a warrant. We would arrest him, and it would be my pleasure to do so. We located where he was living, still with Cathy Jones but not at the condo.

He was an idiot. He had the deal of a lifetime and couldn't stay out of trouble.

He pled guilty and was sentenced to fifteen years. He called me one day and asked me to visit him in jail in Lexington before being transferred to prison out of state. I went, mostly to tell him that I had never known anyone so stupid. The first thing he asked me for was a cigarette. I refused to give him one. He got mad, shouting and cursing. I said my piece and left.

CHAPTER 12:
GOING UNDERCOVER, 1990

During this time, I worked long hours, probably because my relationship with Ann and my children was tense and I did not want to go home. I was completely focused on my work, and because of that I wasn't present for my family. Life in law enforcement takes its toll on our families as well as ourselves. Seeing the completely awful things people do to each other changes cops and FBI agents alike, and I was not immune to that.

Around this time, I decided that I wanted a divorce. Ann didn't agree, but to me the marriage was over. I had been assigned to Headquarters in Washington D.C., and Ann and the children stayed back in Kentucky. At that time, I made the decision to give up a very clear career track to move back to be with them. The irony was that moving back didn't change anything. My children had graduated high school, and while my daughter was doing well, my son was adrift. I'm sure that had something to do with my constant absence, but by this time it was a little late for me to make up for all the hours, days, months, even years I had been off pursuing my passion. I cannot begin to express how saddened I am that I missed the opportunity to be a husband and father—my choice, to be sure—and by this point, there was no going back. It was time for me to be on my own.

I had worked several small undercover cases in my career but nothing long term. While in Harrisburg, I use to tag along with the State Police undercover unit. Thefts, drugs, gambling, and prostitution were some of their exploits. I learned a lot doing this and thought it was fun. I became familiar with the language, what to do and what to say, staying safe and not getting into trouble.

The representatives from the music industry came to our office in Harrisburg asking for help. It seemed the manufacture of bootleg tapes was out of control. We worked the case and ultimately was able to identify the people involved and their location. The people who manufactured the cassettes had machines that could duplicate four at one time. Tapes were sold for $1 to $2 on the black market. The legitimate tapes went for $7 to $8. The estimated loss from violations of copyright laws was in the millions. Once we had all the information we needed, I was sent to Charlotte, North Carolina to meet up with an informant and try to make a buy of a large amount of tapes. I bought ten thousand dollars' worth, and after the buy was made the Charlotte agents raided the building and arrested several suspects.

Another time, as a supervisor in Kentucky, I was sent to Georgia to participate in a Drug Enforcement Agency (DEA) narcotics class. It was a two-week course and I learned a lot about narcotics and the latest drugs of choice. I felt comfortable in my knowledge of the buying of drugs. Years later I was able to use that experience. I had returned to Covington from D.C. and was asked if I would be the undercover operative for a narcotics case that was going to happen in eastern Kentucky. I had the experience and knowledge and I would be able to return home when necessary. The location of the case was in the Pikeville, Prestonburg, and Lexington areas of Kentucky. It was a four-hour drive between eastern Kentucky and Covington so there was little risk of being known or identified as an agent. I would usually travel to the cities on Thursday through Sunday. This is when the action was, and it was the best time to be able to conduct business.

I was given a Cadillac and a two-shot Derringer pistol. I was not sure the Derringer would be able to do much of anything. I rented a condominium and furnished it to make it look as though I was living there full time. The Pikeville office had two agents, Ron Poole and Mark Putnam. Ron was a veteran and Mark was a first office agent. Ron was the major point of contact for me, but Mark talked to me on the telephone if something was needed. I was to let either one of them know my whereabouts and if surveillance was necessary.

Ron Poole introduced me to one of his informants who had been arrested but was trying for a break in his sentence by cooperating with the FBI. Informants are risky but necessary. I talked with this guy for quite some time. I explained to him the rules that I would insist upon: do not get me in a situation I cannot get out of, and do not use any drugs at any time. He was also to tell me who I should be careful with and if any of the people who we were dealing with were armed. From the Bureau's perspective, my life was more important than the bust, and I couldn't agree more.

I worked with another informant in Lexington, Kentucky. He was a former police officer from West Virginia who had been convicted of theft and fired from his position. He seemed like a good guy although I really couldn't trust any informant because I could never know what their motive was. It could be money, consideration in sentencing, or just being a good citizen. It could be ego or narcissism or a thousand other things.

Informants do goofy things sometimes. I had one fellow working as an informant in Harrisburg who was making some good cases for me. He told me he heard there was going to be a hijack of a tractor trailer loaded with seafood. Seafood is a high-dollar item and they said they would kill the driver during the job if necessary. He was asked to help with the hijack and said he would. He kept me informed of their plans.

The suspects met in York, Pennsylvania at 8:00 PM. My informant did not know exactly where they were going and we were told to follow them wherever they went. That was a Saturday and by Monday morning we were in Miami, Florida. We turned the surveillance over to Miami agents. The suspects became suspicious that they were being followed and thought there was someone in the group that was talking with the feds. They suspected my guy. The hijackers left the area and the informant called me and told me he had been tagged as a "rat" and was in danger.

Knowing this we decided to abandon the chance of getting the hijackers and get my guy to a safe place. We returned to Harrisburg and put the informant into the witness protection program. He was in the program for about a year when one day I received a call from someone wanting a reference for a job. The applicant was the informant. Of course, I did not say anything to the hiring person, but I called this guy and told him he was out of the program.

My Lexington informant was a lot savvier than most informants. He knew how to talk and was good at building rapport. We had made a couple of buys in Lexington, cocaine and marijuana, and we ran across a man in a bar who was obviously dealing drugs. Just the way he moved around the bar, I knew something was going on. We struck up a conversation with him and sure enough he asked if we needed anything. I knew what the anything meant. I said not here. He told us he was a male dancer and his group was performing the next night in a bar. I told him I would like to see his performance as I was the owner of a bar and maybe I would bring his group to West Virginia. He liked that.

The next evening, we walked to the entrance of the bar and there was our dealer. There were several men trying to get in as it was ladies' night. He saw we were in line and let us in. We watched part of the show, with the men dancing and stripping. I have never seen a group of women act like that in my life. I went to the restroom. It was very dirty there, and there were the dancers changing costumes. I noticed one of the dancers was snorting cocaine from the top of the urinal. I could not believe it. He looked up and asked me if I wanted to snort some myself. I said no thanks and left. As we were walking out the door, the dancer asked if I wanted anything, meaning cocaine. I said yes and he told me he would see me later that evening. I gave him my number at the hotel where I was staying. It was snowing and I did not think he would show up. At 2:00 AM the phone rang and he asked me to come outside. I did and saw a car driven by a female pull up to where I was standing. The male in the passenger seat motioned me around to his window and handed me a bag of cocaine. As I reached in my pocket to get money to pay, he pulled out a revolver and just held it, letting me know he had a gun.

I made another deal with him two weeks later and the routine was the same except he taped the drugs in a phone booth underneath the shelf.

I met the Lexington informant again at my condo. We discussed and identified the known drug dealers. He knew the names because he had bought cocaine and marijuana from each of them. He also told me where the dealers usually hung out and most of the times it was at a bar. The way this was going to work was that he would contact a dealer to make a buy. If he was successful, he would then introduce the dealer to me, and I would take over making subsequent purchases. This was not a buy-bust operation. If it was, the seller would be arrested immediately. We didn't want to do that because it would be the end of the operation as everyone would know the buyer was law enforcement. We wanted to have at least two to three purchases from as many dealers as we could before any arrests were made.

The informant and I made appearances in several bars in the Pikeville and Prestonsburg areas, meeting and talking with dealers and buyers. My first successful purchase was in Pikeville. A dealer named William was very willing to sell to me as he knew our informant. I bought a small amount of cocaine for $200. He said there was more if I needed it. Once I returned to my condo, I put the cocaine in an evidence bag for the agent handler. I learned later William had been a star basketball player in Pikeville High School and wondered why he was dealing drugs.

I met a lot of people in the bars: men, women, dealers, users, and known crooks. The informant was good about telling me who to talk with and ones I should stay away from. I had to be careful as narcotics dealers are not deacons in the church. They are there to make a lot of money and most of the time don't give a damn if someone gets hurt along the way. One month passed and I felt as though I had become accepted by several people who had access to drug kingpins. Most thought I was an investor from out of town and that I hosted many parties using cocaine and marijuana. My story was that I ran the parties but did not use drugs myself.

I was making several small buys but wanted to get the bigger peddlers. I made contact with an individual named Jim who the informant said was a heavy user, and one to be careful with. Talking with him in a bar, I asked if he had any "blow." That is one of the many terms used for cocaine. The terms changed according to city, county, or state. Cocaine is also called nose candy, snow, and toot, to name just a few. Marijuana is called grass, Mary Jane, skunk, or weed, depending on where you are. It was impossible to keep up with the language.

This dealer said he might have the cocaine I was looking for. He asked how much, and did I have the coupons, meaning cash. I ask him for a half pound. He set the price at $11,000 and I said yes. Jim said he would bring it to my condo the next day.

I had told the informant to come to the condo as I wanted someone else there in case of trouble. Jim showed up at about 2:00 PM. He put a bag of cocaine on the kitchen table, opened it, and said he was going to cook some for us to try. I gave him $11,000 and said we were not going to use it as I was taking it to a party. He insisted, took a small amount of cocaine, cooked it on a spoon, and then free based. I was afraid the informant was going to try it. I gave him a look, and he knew he had better not use or smoke anything. After about an hour Jim finally left and I was relieved. I turned over the cocaine to the agent handler and he later told me it tested to be 95% pure. Pretty good for eastern Kentucky.

One day I ran into a couple who were known dealers and I asked them to stop into my condo someday. A few days later, there was a knock on the door and Sue showed up unannounced. Thank goodness the informant happened to be there with me. Sue came in, sat down, and lit a marijuana cigarette. She asked if we wanted a joint. I told her I did not use anything. We talked for a while and she told me her boyfriend had some good weed if we needed it. I told her I could use some as I was hosting a party in Lexington. She left and said she would return.

The next day she and her boyfriend showed up with a bag of marijuana. I bought it and stored it away. We continued talking and the boyfriend, Joe, told me he was into cockfighting. He raised birds to fight and said he made a lot of money doing this. He said he would take me to watch if I wanted. After they left, I contacted my agent handler and told him of the cockfighting. He in turn contacted the State Police and told them about this. They jumped at the chance to shut the cockfighting down but did not have anyone who could get in. Cockfighting was invitation only and they didn't have anyone close enough to be asked. I had an invitation, though. Joe had told me he would sponsor me, allowing me to enter. I contacted Joe and said I would like to go. Saturday, he came to my condo and said for me to follow him to the cockfight. We drove to a gravel road that was very steep. I had to put the car in first gear to make it up the hill. Reaching the top, I drove up to a gate and stopped. Two men came to my car and asked the name of my sponsor. I told them, and the gate was opened. I was told to drive to the security shed. I was then asked to get out of the car. There, I was photographed and ID'd. After I was checked out, they let me go in. How in the world they had the resources to check my identity I was never able to find out.

I was amazed to see such a facility. It was a real cockfighting ring. I went in and sat down on the bleachers. Two birds with sharp blades attached to their legs were put into the arena. Their handlers or owners let them go and it was awful. Birds trying to kill each other and the people in the stands were cheering on the favorites. Young boys went through the audience soliciting bets, calling "$20 on the red cock or $20 on the white cock." I had never seen this before. I placed a couple of bets as the State Police wanted me to get some evidence, but I had no idea of how to bet and could not identify the bird I bet on. I really did not know how this all worked. The main event was in the large ring. The birds fought until they were just about dead. At some point the owners picked up their birds and went underneath the bleachers. I found this curious and followed them to a smaller arena below the bleachers. This was where the birds were fighting for their life. I watched as one bird was nearly gone, laying on the floor of the arena, blood running out of its mouth. The owner picked up the bird, put his mouth around the head of the bird, and sucked the blood from its mouth. He then put the bird back into the arena to fight again. I had had enough and left. I wrote a report for the State Police and the next Saturday they raided the cockfight, shutting it down and arresting several individuals. Unfortunately, it was up and running again the next week.

I saw Joe and Sue later in the week and bought more cocaine from them. They parked near my condo and wanted me to come to their truck. Joe did not want to hand the cocaine directly to me. He handed the cocaine to Sue who then handed it to me. It was the same for the money. I had to give the money to Sue, and she gave to money to Joe. I guess he thought he couldn't be convicted of dealing if Sue did all the transactions.

I became acquainted with another individual, Larry, who was a dope peddler. I met him at a bar one night and we talked about getting me some nose candy. I asked him if I could get a large amount, and he said he would see what he could get as he wanted some as well. Larry asked me to come out his truck and said, "Do you want to warm your nose?" I just said, "Not now." He said he was going to Florida to see his contact and wanted me to meet him there. I checked with the office in Louisville who authorized me to go. He drove there, and I flew to Miami. I checked in the hotel and met him. We had dinner and he wanted to go to a girlie show, so we found a club and stayed for a while. We returned to the hotel. He said he was going to see his contact the next day and I should to go back to Kentucky and wait for his call. I did not know if he was having second thoughts about me or what.

I returned to Kentucky. A few days later, I received a call from Larry. He said for me to meet him in the parking lot of the Holiday Inn in Lexington. I drove there and waited. One hour passed and Larry pulled into the lot. I got out of my car and walked to where he was parked. He opened the trunk and pulled out a bag of cocaine. I could not believe he was just standing there with what looked like a few pounds of cocaine. I was afraid if we were detected our operation would be over. I gave him $8000, got in my car, and drove back to the condo, securing the cocaine until I could get it to the agent handler. I guess I had passed Larry's test.

Our goal had been to gather enough evidence of drug trafficking that we could get convictions of the higher-ups. We were successful in buying from dope peddlers in the eastern Kentucky region. The operation was winding down and coming to a close. However, there was one dealer that I had not been able to get close enough to to make a buy. I knew Mike did not distribute the cocaine or marijuana himself; instead he had several young women who were his runners. I wanted to get him. By stroke of luck I was in a bar and Mike was there at the same time. It was about midnight. I asked him if I could buy him a drink. Surprisingly he said yes. I believed he had seen me and was told about me being a buyer. We talked for a few minutes and I said I needed some stuff. He wanted to know what kind. I said "blow," and I needed it for a party. He stared a hole through me, and I was trying to keep my trepidation down as much as possible.

He said, "Stay here, I will be back." He returned to the bar in about 15 minutes and said, "Go to Fishtrap Lake at 2:00 AM." I said I would. I went to a phone booth and called my informant and told him what was going on, and that II was going to meet Mike in about an hour. asked where Fishtrap Lake was. He said, "You had better be careful as this is a really bad guy," then he told me how to get to the lake. I found the place and pulled into the parking lot. It was pitch dark and there were no other vehicles around. I backed up to a spot, got out of the car as it was a nice night, and realized the lake was just a short distance from where I had parked. Nothing happened for about ten minutes. Then I saw a car going back and forth in a distant lot. I watched it for a short time and started to get a little leery of what I was seeing. It seemed to be scoping out the area to see if anyone else was there. After all, they would know that I had a lot of money on me if I was buying drugs. My informant was the only person who knew I was there, and my only protection was a two-shot Derringer. I decided this was not worth it, jumped into my car, and sped out of the lot. I passed the other car and I knew it was Mike.

It was time to shut this down, meet with the prosecutors, and make the arrests. Seven arrests were made in one day. All pled guilty except Sue and Joe, the cockfighter. Sue was interviewed with the knowledge she had very little to do with the drugs other than what Joe had told her to do. She agreed to testify for the government and in exchange her charges would be dismissed.

The day came for the trial and the jury was selected and seated. I was a witness, testifying about buying the drugs from Joe. Sue was a very nice, naive person, but was not the queen of the hop. She testified truthfully and did a very good job with the prosecuting attorney. On cross-examination, the defense attorney began questioning Sue. His first question was "How long have you been having an affair with Agent Redden?" With that question, the jury looked at

Sue, looked at me, and the prosecutor turned his head toward me. She responded, "I have never had an affair with Agent Redden." The defense attorney would not give up and asked, "Has Agent Redden ever mentioned sex to you?" She said "No, not even in a joking manner." I turned to the prosecutor and whispered that I wouldn't have approached her for sex "on my worst day." He laughed.

The defense attorney came to me while waiting for the verdict and tried to shake my hand. I said no thanks. The jury came back not guilty. I was not upset with that because I could guess why they felt the way they did.

During my time in the undercover operation, I was working with first office agent Mark Putnam as my handler. Mark was in Pikeville for about a year before he was transferred to Florida. He had an informant, Susan Smith. Mark was married with two children. He began an affair with Susan, and she became pregnant. Mark became desperate and tried to end the relationship while she tried to hang on.

Putnam got his orders to Florida. Susan was very upset and said she was going to the FBI.

Mark moved to Florida, but Susan was trying to still be with Mark. He travelled back to Kentucky and met with Susan It did not go well. Mark had a rental car, and he and Susan drove around talking. It got very heated and Mark strangled Susan Smith to death and threw her down the side of a mountain like a piece of trash. The family demanded answers as her sister knew she was meeting Mark and he was the last person she was seen with. The FBI did not know anything about this for some time but, as soon as they did, Putnam was arrested and convicted. The people of Pikeville became resentful of the FBI and the government after this.

CHAPTER 13:
RETIREMENT, 1995

While I was in Covington, Connie Reid, who was a first office agent, and I had become close. She was not a factor in my divorce—I made sure I cut ties with Ann before Connie and I so much as went on our first date, which was almost a year after the divorce was final—but it was nice to have her around.

In 1991, Connie was transferred to Chicago for her major field office rotation and I remained in Covington. The two cities aren't exactly close, so we maintained a long-distance relationship for a while. On the other hand, this reduced the obvious questions we would have faced if we were in the same office, especially since I was supervisor and she was in her first year.

Connie and I married in 1992. It was no longer convenient for me to be in Covington, and the FBI transferred me to Chicago as a result. I was placed on the Drug Squad but that was not what I wanted to do. I had requested to be on the Bank Robbery Squad but was turned down. The only reason for the drug assignment that I could think of was because of my time working these cases in Kentucky. This was frustrating. I did not want to work drugs anymore as I was tired of dealing with the dirtballs and scumbags who use and sell narcotics. To make matters worse, most cases in Chicago involved Spanish speakers and I did not speak the language. Another complicating factor was that I was not used to working on a squad with a single focus. I was used to working different cases as you do in a resident agency. It wasn't the teamwork that bothered me. I had always been a team player. But I had become used to the variety, and working drugs was frustrating. But, as I had done in the past, I did not say anything. There was nothing to say.

Chicago was a different place. It was a big city with heavy traffic. Unlike Covington or even Harrisburg, it was difficult to get around, and there was lots of crime. On the other hand, it had some good restaurants if you could get in. Connie wasn't happy with her assignment any more than I was. She is an accountant so they placed her on the Bankruptcy Squad. This was not very exciting for her as she was also used to the variety of different cases in Covington.

Connie had two horses she had shipped to Chicago and I bought a horse there. We began competing and worked with a trainer who taught us both how to ride dressage and how to jump. Connie was a good rider and I was a rookie but we both worked hard to be able to show and compete. We were spending nights and weekends driving an hour to where the horses were boarded. We were paying more to board the horses than we were paying for our condominium on Lake Shore Drive overlooking Lake Michigan.

Our first competition we entered was stressful. Connie was doing well, but I was eliminated. I could not get my horse to go over the jump, so the judge whistled me off the arena. I was not going to let that happen again. I trained for another whole year and entered again. I came in first place and Connie placed first in her division. We both had the same trainer and he couldn't believe we both won first place. The next one I entered, I came in first place again. Connie finished third. We both enjoyed this and competed at several other events.

At this time, I was thinking about retirement. We began searching for farms as we wanted to raise horses to sell and not have the boarding expense. Farms in Illinois were very expensive and the prices kept pushing us farther away from northern Illinois. Finally, we found a farm in Wisconsin that we could afford. The place was a disaster, completely run down. The house had been built in 1860, and was occupied by a lady who bought the farm and acreage in an auction. The second floor was uninhabitable, and the first was not much better. Connie had the vision and thought it might work. I was clueless as I knew my handyman skills were not up to the task. The truth of the matter was that I could barely swing a hammer, forget hitting a nail.

We made a ridiculously low offer for the farm and, to my surprise, the woman countered my offer. I knew we were in the ballpark and increased the offer. She took it. We went to a bank in Monroe, Wisconsin for financing. I had enough for a down payment, but much was needed to fix the place. Both of our parents thought we were crazy, and one said just bulldoze it down and start over. The bank officer was great. He agreed to help us with the repairs and gave us the name of a good carpenter. The manager said just bring the bills to him and it would be added to the mortgage.

We both were still living in Chicago and coming out on the weekends and our vacation time. I decided to retire—this was my 24th year—and Connie resigned as we wanted to spend time fixing the house. My son Jason was living in Cincinnati and was having trouble in his life. I drove to Ohio and brought him to our house in the hope that we might be able to help him. Regardless of our divorce, Ann and I banded together for Jason. It worked for a while, but he eventually returned to Cincinnati and his troubles continued. Ann, Connie, and I did everything we could do, but he was in the wrong crowd. Whatever he needed, we just couldn't provide.

Connie and I worked on the house for two years, making many changes and repairs. The carpenter said we basically rebuilt the house from the inside out. The work is finished for the time being. It is comfortable and looks good, but there is always something to do or fix.

I became restless. I obtained a teacher's license and began substitute teaching in the local schools. I enjoyed this for a while and the kids liked hearing my FBI stories. I had been doing this for about two years when I noticed an ad in the newspaper that was recruiting for a fraud prevention manager. I answered the ad and received an interview. It was an insurance company with a Medicare contract. I got the job, supervising fraud cases in four states. This went very well and eventually Connie got a job at the same company in a different division.

My investigators were very good, and one case made big news. One guy in the Chicago office telephoned me and said he had come across a podiatrist who was billing Medicare for a lot of money. He said it was not possible to bill for as many services as the doctor was submitting. I told him to get the report out as soon as he could.

It was a lot of data that had to be researched and it took about six months to complete the investigation. It turned out that Doctor Mikos was billing over one million dollars a year. He would go to nursing homes and clip the toenails of the residents and then charge Medicare as if it was a surgery. We turned the case over to Department of Health agents for subsequent charges.

Mikos was indicted and arrested, and let out on bail. We learned Mikos was on drugs, had many women at his side, and was a heavy gambler. Mikos had all the names of the witnesses. One of the witnesses, a beneficiary of Medicare, was scheduled to testify before the grand jury. Mikos went to that woman, who was in a wheelchair and lived in a basement apartment in a church. He told her to change her testimony. When she refused, he shot and killed her. The agents were able to identify him as the shooter and he was convicted of both murder and fraud. He now sits on death row.

Meanwhile, Connie began managing investigators at a property and casualty (P&C) company. The place I was working subsequently lost their Medicare contract. All my investigators and I were in limbo wondering if we were going to have a job or not. I was able to place most of them in other positions in the company. Then I took a job in the education division of Connie's company.

While working in the P&C, I had the opportunity to study to get a Ph.D. This had been a goal of mine for a long time but financially had been out of my reach. This company offered compensation for anyone who was interested in a higher education. Between that compensation and the help from my parents, I was able to enter a good school. It was tough—actually, "tough" doesn't really do it justice; perhaps "brutal" would be more accurate—but I hung in there. I got to the point in my life where I was not able to keep up with work, travel, and my Ph.D. studies. I decided to retire for the third time and work only on getting the Ph.D.

One week after I retired, I received a phone call from a friend of mine asking me if I would come to work for him. The company had a Medicare contract and needed management people. I said yes as they would let me work from home two days a week. I would travel to Denver and Nashville the other days. My job was to accompany nurses and investigators making unannounced on-site visits to review medical records and Medicare billing.

We travelled to Atlanta to visit a medical clinic. It was in a poor area, the place was filthy, and the records were almost non-existent. Given the amount and type of Medicare billing we saw coming from this place, it was obvious there was fraud going on. I called the Medicare office in Maryland and asked for them to shut it down. They did but it took a year.

I was able to keep up my Ph.D. work and finally graduated in 2009. My only regret was my father had passed away three months before graduation. My mother, my brother and his wife, and Connie were there, and it was great day. I never thought I would make it.

My brother, Paul, was a sheriff in Buffalo, Wyoming. When his term was over, he went to San Diego where he became a polygraph examiner. He retired as chief polygraph examiner and now lives with his wife Sharon in Albuquerque, New Mexico. He worked some really high-profile cases and has travelled to foreign countries teaching their law enforcement officers how to interview and use the polygraph.

My son Jason was still having problems and I was pulling my hair out. I wanted to help him but it wasn't easy. I'm sure he wanted to get out of his situation, but he sure didn't act like it. I wish I could have been as supportive of him as my parents were of me, but by that time Jason had become so distant that there wasn't anything I could do but put him in God's hands. I hope every day that we can be a family again. Jason might question whether we had been a family in the first place. To be fair, he may have something there.

My daughter, LeeAnn, has not spoken to me since the divorce. I have tried many times to make amends and to see her children. She is adamant that she won't talk to me. I have never once seen my grandchildren. It bothers me terribly, but there's nothing I can do about it. Both my grandchildren are tremendous athletes. One is playing football for the U.S. Air Force Academy. I really don't know what my other grandchild is doing now. This weighs on me every day.

Jason is doing well now, and I just hope he can make something of himself. He's been adrift for so long, like I was before finding myself in the FBI. I got lucky. I hope he has the same kind of luck.

Recently, Ann was diagnosed with breast cancer and became very sick. I met with her several times before she passed away in Cincinnati. I was so glad we reconnected. Even though I was absolutely terrible at showing it, I loved her and my family more than I can express.

Today, Connie and I raise horses, both thoroughbreds and warm bloods. We now have ninety-five acres, fourteen horses, chickens, cats, peacocks, and a collie named Beau.